THE HOLIDAY CANDY BOOK

THE HOLIDAY
Candy Book

BY VIRGINIA PASLEY

DRAWINGS BY BARBARA CORRIGAN

COACHWHIP PUBLICATIONS
Greenville, Ohio

To
Fred

The Holiday Candy Book, by Virginia Pasley
© 2024 Coachwhip Publications edition

First published 1952
Virginia Pasley, 1905-1986
CoachwhipBooks.com
Original cover design by Barbara Corrigan

ISBN 1-61646-591-3
ISBN-13 978-1-61646-591-9

Acknowledgments

My thanks to the children of Massapequa Park, who beat a path to our door in their eagerness to be of assistance in tasting our test candies, and also to my colleagues at the newspaper *Newsday,* who were equally co-operative. But most of all I want to thank my sister Eleanor, Mrs. James Lichtgarn, whose part in preparing and writing this book made it possible.

VIRGINIA PASLEY

Contents

Contents

Contents

Contents

Contents

THE HOLIDAY CANDY BOOK

Candy Is Fun

FROM the first lollipop at the first children's party to the gold-wrapped cherry cordial at a golden anniversary all of the festive occasions of a lifetime are associated with candy. There is no holiday that is not enhanced by candy and if it isn't a holiday, candy will make it one.

There are the candies that set off every holiday throughout the year: candied popcorn stars and marzipan strawberries at Christmas time, pink and red hearts on Valentine's Day, chocolate-covered eggs at Easter time, marshmallows to roast at the Fourth of July picnic and candied fruits and nuts on Thanksgiving Day.

Is there anything as delicious, as tempting or as satisfying as a piece of candy? There is the penny candy of our extreme youth — "I'll take one of these and two of those and one of these" — choosing after solemn deliberation; the excitement over the candy apples on a stick when autumn comes; the wonderful if grimy mess of a childhood taffy pull; the first box of candy presented awkwardly by a speechless, gangling beau.

Candy tastes good and is good. And it tastes much better and is much better if you make it yourself. Whatever your favorite candy, whether butter crunch or fudge, nougat or molasses taffy, peanut brittle or chocolate mint patties, you can make it better than the best candy you ever bought. You can even learn to make fancy-dipped chocolates and bonbons that look as tempting as the ones you gazed at longingly as a child with your nose pressed against the confectioner's plate-glass window. And they'll live up to their looks, if you make them yourself.

If you feel the candy you've been eating isn't as good as it used to be, don't ascribe it to the tricks that memories of the good old days play on you. You've just not been eating the right candy. Homemade candy is better than ever. Try it and see.

As youngsters at home my sister and I made fudge and penuche, fondant and divinity, taffy to pull and popcorn balls, and occasionally even dipped dates and nuts in chocolate. We tried to make marshmallows but there was something wrong with our recipes or our equipment and they always turned out with a layer of gelatin on the bottom. We experimented with caramels but had not the patience to cook them as long as was needed in the recipes that we found. And we never, never could make butter crunch without having it separate.

We continued to make a few of our old favorites, stirring up fudge once in a while in the middle of the night when a gnawing sweet tooth was unable to discover a single piece of candy around the house to appease it. But we felt for many years that most candy was something to be made by the experts — which we weren't.

Well, we know differently now and we think that what we have learned will make it possible for you, too, to make candy as good as any of the experts — and without tears.

We found, for instance, that butter crunch won't separate if it's cooked in a heavy skillet instead of a saucepan. That caramels can be made by a new method which cuts the cooking time as much as $2\frac{1}{2}$ hours. That even chocolate dipping, admittedly the fussiest of candymaking processes, is easy to conquer when you recognize that chocolate demands certain conditions and won't behave, otherwise. Sugar itself, though not as cranky as chocolate, follows the rules of its own chemistry and does not take kindly to attempts to change those rules.

The special value of these candy recipes is that, whether they're old standard recipes or new ones we created, they are fresh enough to us so that we take nothing for granted — so often the case when you've made a recipe for years on end and forgotten the difficulties you encountered the first time you made it.

On the other hand, in talking to candy enthusiasts who were always ready to test our samples we discovered that the candy considered best by the experts is not always so regarded by their public. Al-most everyone has tried his hand at making chocolate fudge, and nothing in the world has ever tasted so good as that fudge you whipped up just because you wanted something sweet and lovely. Purists say that fudge of yours was probably pretty poor stuff and all modern cookbooks have recipes that correct its bad features. By the new methods you can produce a delicious soft creamy fudge, of the consistency of fondant but not at all like the hard and grainy stuff you made in mother's kitchen or over the spirit lamp at college. Yet, it's not the expert's creamy fudge that many of us want at all, but the kind of fudge that tastes like home and childhood — and since many have now lost the knack of making "bad" fudge we include in this book directions for making both creamy fudge and old-fashioned "amateur" fudge.

To make candy is to assist at a miracle. Starting with sugar and water you can make fondant, white taffy, lollipops and barley sugar merely by boiling the syrup to higher and higher temperatures and adding flavoring. The change that takes place with each degree is the miracle.

If you add milk, or butter, or cream, or chocolate you widen the range to include fudge and caramels, butterscotch and toffee; add an egg white and you get nougat or divinity; some gelatin and you have marshmallows or jellies.

Of course that's not the whole story. It's what you do to the sugar syrup at every stage, as well as temperature variations, that decides the texture or quality of your candy.

If you wanted to eat plain sugar, you wouldn't bother to make candy. One of your chief concerns will be to see that your candy doesn't turn back into sugar. That's why it is important to add to sugar syrups an ingredient that slows down crystallization — such as corn syrup, cream of tartar, or an acid such as lemon juice or vinegar. That's also why most of the candies that have few ingredients besides sugar and water are not stirred after reaching the boiling point — because it has been discovered that stirring can start off a chain reaction and cause your candy to crystallize.

When you're making this type of candy, especially fondant and hard candies, sugar crystals that form on the sides of the pan are washed away with a fork wrapped in muslin or a pastry brush, dipped in hot water.

It's important to read through an entire recipe before you begin to make your candy. Then you will know just what equipment to use, how long the process will take, how much attention you need to give it at each stage, and whether you can take time out to peel the potatoes for supper. In making candy, timing is as important as it is in a comedy act. Doing the right thing at the right moment according to the readings of your thermometer is what will ensure consistent success for your efforts.

Equipment for candymaking need not be elaborate, but *must* include a candy thermometer if you expect good results. Cold-water tests for each stage of candymaking have been developed; but even when used by the experienced, they cover too wide a range for accuracy (the beginner cannot tell with any assurance the difference between a hard soft ball and a soft hard ball).

You will also need saucepans ranging from one to four quarts in size, if you are to make all the varieties;

candy thermometer

a wooden spoon for stirring or beating; a slab or platter for cooling candies that are to be worked; pans to set your candy; waxed paper or cellophane for wrapping, and tin boxes for storing.

But there are really only three essentials for becoming an expert candy cook — a candy thermometer, a willingness to do precisely what must be done if the sugar and chocolate in your batches are to stay under control, and recipes that are detailed enough so you will know what must be done and how and when to do it.

The first you can buy, the second is up to you, and I hope that in this little book we have supplied the third.

General Directions

Type of Candy	Stage Desired	Degrees F.	Cold-Water Test
Fondant Fudges Penuche	Soft ball	234 to 240	Forms soft ball which flattens out
Caramels	Hard ball	244 to 250	Forms hard ball which does not flatten
Divinity Taffy	Extra-hard ball	250 to 265	Forms very hard ball which holds its shape
Toffee Butter crunch Nougat syrup	Soft crack	270 to 290	Separates into threads which are hard but not brittle
Butterscotch Brittle Glacé Basic hard candy	Hard crack	300 to 310	Separates into threads which are hard and brittle
Caramelized sugar		over 310	No cold-water test — sugar liquefies and caramelizes

To make the cold-water tests drop a small amount of the candy you are cooking from the end of a spoon into a large cup of really cold water. As your tests show you are approaching the proper stage, remove the candy from the heat.

READING A THERMOMETER

With a candy thermometer you can be sure you have reached exactly the right degree of temperature for the particular candy you are making. But the thermometer must be read correctly, with your eye right on the level of the top of the mercury, not above or below.

TESTING YOUR THERMOMETER

Test your thermometer by placing it in a pan of water and bringing it to the boiling point. It should now register 212° at sea level. If it registers 214° you can correct it by adding two degrees to those given in the recipe; if 210°, by subtracting. If it is more than a few degrees off in either direction, you need a new thermometer.

CORRECTING THE THERMOMETER FOR ALTITUDE

For every thousand feet above sea level subtract roughly two degrees from the suggested thermometer readings. For example, if you are making fondant in the mountains and the altitude is 4000 feet, instead of cooking it up to 238° you would remove it from the heat when the thermometer registers 230°.

CORRECTING FOR HUMID OR RAINY WEATHER

When the barometric pressure is low or the weather is rainy or humid, cook most candies two degrees higher than you would normally.

HARD WATER

If your water is unusually hard it may make the difference between success and failure in your candy-making. Boil one gallon of hard water with a teaspoon of soda for twenty minutes, to neutralize, before using water to make candy.

STORING CANDY

All candy should be kept in a cool place and most should be packed in tin boxes for best keeping. Caramels should always be wrapped soon after cutting to prevent spreading.

CHANGING RECIPES

Proportions in these recipes are carefully worked out for best results and usually should not be changed. Increasing the amount of liquid, for instance, will lengthen the cooking time and give a less tender result. Recipes can be doubled successfully in almost every instance but in that case a larger saucepan must be used or the candy will boil over or cook too slowly. Cutting recipes in half is not advisable because very small quantities are difficult to work with. For a few large quantity recipes see pages 112 to 116.

EQUIPMENT FOR THE CANDYMAKER

Candy thermometer	3-quart saucepan
Measuring cups and spoons	4-quart saucepan
1-quart saucepan	Heavy 12-inch skillet

General Directions

Double boiler
Wooden spoons
Pastry brush or muslin-
    wrapped fork
Fondant paddle
Marble slab or large platter
Chocolate grater
Standard beaters, wire
    whisks

Electric beater
Pans, 8 by 11 inch, 7 by 7
    inch
Cookie sheets
Funnel and stick
Heavy, sharp knife
Waxed paper
Cellophane
Tin boxes for storing

Winter Holidays

WHEN there's snow on the ground and the air is crisp outside, candymaking is more fun than usual. That's why so many of us make so much candy around Christmas time. Even the words "Christmas candy" have a magical quality. Candied popcorn wreaths and stars, Santa Claus lollipops, candy canes, and the fascinating colored and shaped marzipan dainties belong to the Christmas season. But your Christmas candymaking will not be confined to these seasonal specialties alone. Winter weather gives the candymaker her best break for all her favorite candies. Everything turns out right when the humidity is down and the weather is cool. So make all your best varieties for Christmas and New Year's, not just for the family but to pack in boxes or tins to give to fortunate friends.

The winter season also brings the sweetest day of all — St. Valentine's Day — which would not be the same without candy. For this holiday dedicated to lovers, make your favorite candies in heart shapes, out of pink fondant or bright-red hard candy or clear-cerise jelly candies. For the children, make anise-flavored lollipops decorated with icing hearts pierced with arrows. And for That Special Person, assemble an array of luscious chocolates and bonbons, add samples of your other favorites and pack it in a red-satin heart box.

Washington's Birthday is another occasion for special efforts in candymaking. Glacéed or candied cherries or red hard candies flavored with cherry are good choices, as are old-fashioned candies such as barley-sugar twists which were made and eaten with relish as far back as Revolutionary days. For a special party, decorate fondant patties with little hatchets made of royal icing, colored, and squeezed out of a pastry tube.

CANDIED POPCORN IN FANCY SHAPES

1 cup sugar	2 tablespoons butter
⅓ cup light corn syrup	¼ teaspoon salt
⅓ cup water	1 teaspoon vanilla
2 quarts popped corn	

Measure 1 cup sugar, ⅓ cup light corn syrup, ⅓ cup water and 2 tablespoons butter into a saucepan and blend well together. Place over low heat and stir until mixture boils. Now put in the candy thermometer and continue boiling without stirring until thermometer registers 270°. Remove from heat and add ¼ teaspoon salt and 1 teaspoon vanilla. Have ready

a bowl of freshly popped corn — about 8 cups will be sufficient for the amount of syrup cooked. Pour the hot syrup over the popcorn stirring well and quickly so that all the kernels are covered. Popcorn balls can be formed if desired. Moisten the hands with cold water and quickly take a small amount of the candied corn and gently press into a ball. If other shapes such as Christmas trees, stars and wreaths are to be made, molds or cookie cutters may be used. A large pan molded in Christmas-tree form can be found at most department stores. Press the candied corn into the mold, making sure that the corn is in all the small parts of the design. While the candied popcorn is still warm, place small pieces of colored candies to resemble the ornaments on a tree. Red and green colors are most effective and will make the popcorn Christmas tree a gay centerpiece for a children's holiday party. For wreaths and stars the candied corn is pressed in the cookie cutters. The points of the stars must be well filled to have the formation distinct. A doughnut cutter is good for the wreath, with colored pieces of candy added for holiday festiveness. If the candied corn becomes too hard to work into the molds, it may be placed in a warm oven and softened.

For caramel corn use any preferred caramel recipe, cooking only to 242°. This will be stickier and is not good for molding into shapes.

FONDANT

When Mother got out her marble slab and let us help her make fondant we felt as though we were being let in on a really exciting process. For in making fondant, what is one moment just runny sugar syrup changes under your hands and before your eyes into a thick, opaque, creamy candy. And fondant is the basis for mints and bonbons and myriad chocolate-cream centers that can be your proudest candies.

The directions for making fondant sound formidable, and plain fondant, which is where many cooks stop, is not the most interesting candy you can turn out. But making fondant is much simpler than it sounds, because the directions are so explicit; and when you have added colorings and flavors, or tried butter creams and flowing Oriental creams, you will no longer find fondant dull.

You do not need a marble slab or a wooden paddle to make good fondant; a platter or a large plate will do instead of the marble, and a spatula can be used instead of a wooden paddle. But if you have a marble slab by all means use it, because the fondant will cool more quickly.

Following the directions is important in any candy but you will see the results of mistakes more spectacularly in fondant. The rules that say you should stir the sugar and water while it is dissolving and then must not stir again after it boils are not made to cause you trouble but to keep you from having it. Washing the crystals from the side of the pan is equally important, as is allowing the candy to cool down to approximately 110° before beginning to cream it. All of these seemingly fussy directions are aimed at one thing: to keep your candy from sugaring off, from getting grainy, and to make sure that it will be smooth and creamy when it is finished.

For the same reason you need to be careful not to jar the pan when you are taking it off the stove or the platter or slab on which it is cooling. And when you pour the candy out onto the platter do not scrape the sides or attempt to shake out the last few drops.

Basic fondant is one of the simplest of candies. Sugar and water alone will make a passable fondant if all precautions are taken to keep it from sugaring. But to ensure success a small amount of acid or corn syrup is nearly always added. We use cream of tartar in most of our fondant recipes but if you find you have none on your shelf when you start to make fondant you can substitute a half teaspoon of lemon juice or two tablespoons of corn syrup in place of an eighth of a teaspoon of cream of tartar.

Fondant must be aged or mellowed for most purposes. Often an hour is long enough, but check the recipe you want to make so you're not disappointed to find that you cannot finish your candy until the next day.

BASIC FONDANT

2 cups sugar   ¾ cup boiling water
⅛ teaspoon cream of tartar

Measure 2 cups sugar and ¾ cup boiling water into a 2-quart saucepan. Blend with a wooden spoon, and place over low heat, stirring continuously until the mixture begins to dissolve. Continue stirring until the mixture boils, then add ⅛ teaspoon cream of tartar. Cover for 3 minutes so that steam may wash down and melt any sugar crystals on sides of the pan. Uncover and put in your candy thermometer. With a fork wrapped with muslin and moistened in warm water wash off any further sugar crystals that form during cooking. Or you can use a moistened pastry brush. Always use an upward movement. Boil without stirring over medium-high heat until the thermometer registers 238°. Remove from heat, being careful not to jar the pan, and let stand until all bubbles have disappeared. Pour carefully onto a marble slab or a large tray or platter that has been moistened and cooled in the refrigerator, so that the fondant may cool as quickly as possible. Pour only what leaves

the pan easily. Do not scrape sides of pan or shake
out remaining candy. When it feels only slightly
warm to the touch (about 110°), work the candy over
and over with a scraping and folding method using
a wooden paddle or a spatula. As the candy thickens
it becomes opaque and when finished it forms a hard
crumbly white mass, and can no longer be worked
with the paddle. At this point kneading it with the
hands brings about the desired softness and the candy
is ready to be ripened for chocolate centers, bonbons
or mint patties. Cover with a damp cloth and store in
a jar at room temperature. Flavoring and coloring are
added after the fondant is ripened. For bonbons and
mint patties fondant should be used after two days
of ripening. (For chocolate dipping, see pages 32–37.)

MINT PATTIES

1 recipe basic fondant (*page*   1 teaspoon peppermint ex-
    22)   tract
Pink, green or yellow coloring

Melt fondant in a double boiler over hot water,
stirring gently, until it is the consistency of very heavy
cream. Carefully, without too much stirring, add 1
teaspoon of peppermint extract, and desired coloring.
Fondant may be divided into portions and each

The Holiday Candy Book

colored with a different color. Drop by teaspoonfuls on waxed paper or use a warmed funnel and wooden stick. When cool these may be decorated with royal icing or dipped in chocolate.

BUTTER CREAMS

2 cups sugar	1/8 teaspoon cream of tartar
3/4 cup boiling water	3 tablespoons butter

Measure 2 cups sugar and 3/4 cup boiling water into a 2-quart saucepan. Blend with a wooden spoon, and place over low heat, stirring continuously until the mixture begins to dissolve. Continue stirring until it boils, then add 1/8 teaspoon cream of tartar. Cover for 3 minutes so that steam may wash down and melt any sugar crystals on sides of the pan. Uncover and put in your candy thermometer. With a fork wrapped with muslin and moistened in warm water wash off any further sugar crystals that form during cooking. Boil without stirring over medium-high heat until the thermometer registers 238°. Remove from heat and let candy stand until all bubbles have disappeared. Pour on a marble slab or on a large tray or platter that has been moistened and cooled in the refrigerator. It is important that the syrup cool as quickly as

[24]

possible. When it feels only slightly warm to the touch (about 110°) add 3 tablespoons softened butter and work the candy over and over with a scraping and folding method using a wooden paddle or a spatula. As the candy thickens it becomes opaque and when finished it forms a crumbly mass and can no longer be worked with the paddle. At this point kneading it with the hands brings about the desired softness and the candy is ready to be flavored, colored and molded for chocolate dipping (see pages 32–37). No ripening is necessary. Store in refrigerator if not used the same day.

ORIENTAL CREAMS

2 cups sugar	⅛ teaspoon cream of tartar
¾ cup boiling water	1 egg white (medium size)
½ teaspoon glycerin	Flavorings and colorings

Measure 2 cups sugar and ¾ cup boiling water into a 2-quart saucepan. Blend with a wooden spoon and place over low heat, stirring continuously until the mixture begins to dissolve. Now add ½ teaspoon glycerin and ⅛ teaspoon cream of tartar and continue stirring until the mixture boils. Cover for 3 minutes so that steam may wash down and melt any sugar crystals on sides of the pan. Uncover and put in your candy thermometer. With a fork wrapped with muslin and moistened in warm water wash off any further sugar crystals that form during cooking. Boil without stirring over medium-high heat until the thermometer registers 238°. Remove from heat and let candy stand until all bubbles have disappeared. Pour on a marble slab or on a large tray or platter that has been moistened and cooled in refrigerator. When candy feels only slightly warm to the touch (about 110°), add the stiffly beaten egg white, spreading it over the top of the syrup, then work the candy over and over with a scraping and folding method using a wooden paddle or a spatula. As the candy thickens it becomes white and creamy. Work for at least 10 minutes, then scrape together and let set, covered with waxed paper, until thick enough to mold into shapes for dipping. If a variety of flavors is desired the fondant may be divided into four parts: one part flavored with vanilla, the second part with mint, the third with lemon extract and colored with a small amount of yellow color and the last with raspberry extract and colored with a very small amount of red. After the candy is formed into balls for dipping it is left to dry in a cool room. When a very thin crust has formed the creams are ready to be dipped (see pages 32–37). If allowed to stand too long they become runny and very difficult to handle with the soft chocolate. The flavor is improved if the chocolates are allowed to ripen for a few days after dipping. The purpose of the glycerin is to keep the cream center moist and very soft.

UNCOOKED FONDANT

1 egg white   2 tablespoons water
3 cups confectioners' sugar

Mix 1 egg white with 2 tablespoons water and then add gradually 3 cups confectioners' sugar. Flavoring, coloring and nuts may be added when the fondant is formed for dipping. This is a quick substitute for cooked fondant though it is never as creamy and smooth to the taste.

FONDANT FOR COATING

2 cups sugar   ⅛ teaspoon cream of tartar
¾ cup boiling water   ½ teaspoon glycerin

Here the method is the same as for basic fondant, but add ½ teaspoon of glycerin to the sugar and

The Holiday Candy Book

water mixture at the start of the cooking. This addition of glycerin keeps the bonbon coating soft and also gives it a glossy finish. After the fondant has ripened at least 4 hours and no more than 48 hours, melt the fondant over water that has been brought to the boiling point. Care has to be taken so that the fondant does not become too hot or too dry. Warm water or a stock syrup of equal parts water and sugar that has been heated to 220° may be added if the fondant appears too thick. It is also possible for the fondant to become too moist and runny. If this happens keep fondant over hot water to dry it out. For coating centers with fondant, the consistency has to be just right. The center to be coated is placed on a fork and quickly dipped into the melted fondant. When covered it is lifted out and placed on waxed paper and the excess string is used to form a curlicue or a pattern indicating the type of center dipped. Practice will soon help the dipper know when the fondant is right for coating centers. Butter creams, chocolate and vanilla, marzipan, coconut mixed with fondant, apricot paste, jelly squares and fruit mixtures all make good centers for bonbons. The fondant for coating can also be flavored and colored in many different ways.

Winter Holidays

ROYAL ICING

| 2 egg whites | 1 teaspoon lemon juice |
| 1/8 teaspoon cream of tartar | 1 pound confectioners' sugar |

Beat together the whites of 2 eggs, 1/8 teaspoon cream of tartar and 1 teaspoon lemon juice just enough to blend well. Gradually add 1 pound confectioners' sugar, beating until the mixture is stiff and will not drop from the spoon. Less than a pound of sugar may be sufficient if the egg whites are smaller than average. Beating time will usually be 7 or 8 minutes. This icing is used for decorating bonbons, Easter eggs, lollipops and mints and may be colored with vegetable colorings. Feed through a pastry tube using attachments of various sizes to make rosettes, leaves, etc., and to write names on Easter eggs.

CRYSTALLIZING

| 2 cups sugar | 1 cup water |
| Brown paper | |

Blend 2 cups sugar and 1 cup water in a 2-quart saucepan. Place over medium heat and stir until mixture boils. Put in your candy thermometer and continue cooking without stirring until the temperature reaches 225°. Remove from heat. Cut a small hole in

The Holiday Candy Book

the center of a piece of brown paper larger than the
pan. Dampen the paper with cold water and gently
lay it on top of the sugar syrup, being careful to fit it
closely around the sides of the pan. Allow to cool until
lukewarm. Remove the paper and any crystals which
have formed.

Meanwhile place the candies — fondant or jellies
(see pages 19–27, 64–70) in fancy shapes or colors
— which are to be crystallized on racks in pans deep
enough so that they can be covered with the syrup.
Pour the syrup over them and place a piece of muslin
over the top. Allow to stand for twelve hours. Remove
the candies from the syrup, place on dry racks and allow to dry in a warm room for another twelve hours.
The surface of the candies will be covered with bright
sugar crystals. Bonbons and jellied candies are usually
crystallized by this method. They keep better and
look gayer, but the process is long and requires proper
drying racks. This recipe may be doubled or tripled,
using a larger saucepan in that case.

Marzipan

Marzipan is especially associated with the Christmas season, and if you have a talent for sculpture you
can use it here.

Winter Holidays

The colorings may be painted on the finished shapes instead of being mixed with all the marzipan. In this case dilute the coloring with water until you get the desired shade.

Favorite shapes are strawberries, carrots, pears and apples. Potatoes are formed and rolled in cocoa instead of being colored. Faces are fun, too, the eyes fashioned by making indentations with toothpicks.

MARZIPAN (uncooked)

2 cups blanched almonds   1 cup confectioners' sugar
   (finely grated or ground)   or more
                    ¼ cup egg whites

Grate or grind 2 cups almonds very fine, work in a wooden bowl with a wooden spoon, and add 1 cup confectioners' sugar alternately with ¼ cup egg whites, using more sugar if necessary to form a stiff paste. Allow to ripen a few hours before coloring and forming into fancy shapes. Or use it for centers for chocolate dipping or roll in cocoa. This does not keep well.

MARZIPAN WITH FONDANT

¾ pound almond paste *or*
  1 recipe uncooked mar-
  zipan (*page 31*)

1 cup fondant
¼ cup light corn syrup

Mix ¾ pound almond paste (or use the uncooked marzipan described above) with 1 cup basic fondant and ¼ cup light corn syrup and knead until smooth. Allow to ripen. Color and form into fancy shapes.

CHOCOLATES AND CHOCOLATE DIPPING

The best compliment that can be paid store-bought candy is to say it tastes homemade. This is as true of chocolates as it is of any other candy, but the proudest compliment a home chocolate dipper can receive is to have someone say her chocolates *look* professional — though they must still taste homemade.

Chocolate dipping is a profession and dippers spend much time becoming adept at it, but once you have learned about the temperature requirements, the actual dipping is not difficult.

Regular coating chocolate comes only in ten-pound slabs and can usually be bought only at wholesale houses, although sometimes a local bakery may be willing to sell you some as a favor. However, you can use semisweet chocolate for dipping, the milk chocolate that is broken from big bars and sold at the ten-cent store or, if you like a bitter chocolate coating over a rich butter cream, you can even use regular baking chocolate.

cacao tree
and pod with
cocoa beans

Whatever type you use, you may be surprised, if you have casually melted chocolate over boiling water or even over direct heat for cakes, cookies or frostings, to find that it is extremely sensitive to temperatures and to the way it is handled at any given stage. If chocolate is allowed to get too hot, or cools too quickly without being beaten, it will refuse to harden, it will harden in gray streaks, or it will come out in spots.

To find out why this happens we went to see a chemist for one of the big chocolate companies. He had helped earn his college tuition by working as a chocolate dipper so he knew chocolate dipping from both the scientific and practical points of view.

Professional candymakers call those gray streaks that appear even on their chocolates "bloom," and they haven't completely licked the problem themselves. When I told him that sometimes the chocolate hardened on my fingers while I was dipping he peered at me earnestly.

"Are you anemic?" he asked. "Chocolate dippers have to be strong and healthy — and they wear red flannels."

This is because chocolate dipping must be done in a cool room if it is to be completely successful. And the gray streaks or spots appear because in chocolate there are various types of fat globules with different hardening temperatures. Unless they are kept in motion right up to the moment when chocolate as a whole will solidify, the fat will harden separately from the rest of the components.

To get around this, chocolate used in dipping is never allowed to get hotter than 125° and it is better if it does not get over 110°. It is kept in motion while it is cooling and the dipping is done in a cold room, 60° to 65°, so that the chocolate coating will harden before the fat globules can separate again.

chocolate dipping

Use at least a pound of chocolate for one session of dipping, shave it finely and put it in the top of a double boiler over water no higher than 120° measured on your candy thermometer. Cover the chocolate and begin to get your centers ready for dipping. Stir occasionally so that the heat is distributed evenly. When most of the chocolate is melted beat it thoroughly with a spoon or rubber paddle, smoothing out all the lumps.

In the meantime have the candies you are going to dip lined up on a board or tin in the room where you are to dip them. Spread waxed paper or oilcloth over your work surface or use a marble slab.

Professional dippers grease a section of the marble slab, pour out part of the chocolate and work it with their fingers until it is the right consistency and the right temperature. We found it easier to put part of the chocolate into a pie tin which could then be moved on and off a pan of warm water, depending on whether it was beginning to get too cool or too warm. As needed, more chocolate is added from the double boiler.

The right temperature for dipping, according to authorities, is about 83°. But the chocolate dipper cannot easily measure the chocolate at this thick stage with a thermometer and must learn to recognize the right stage by dipping test pieces.

If they harden in a minute or two the chocolate is probably just right. If they develop gray streaks or dots it isn't. If they spread out and you cannot form a design on top that doesn't melt away, the chocolate is too warm. In practice it is surprising how quickly you can begin to tell by touch when the right moment has come. The chocolate should begin to feel cool to your fingers and seem to thicken slightly under them.

Dipping forks may be used instead of the fingers

but while it may sound easier and certainly is less messy, there are many objections to it. Finger dipping is the best and quickest way for the amateur to become a professional.

SUGGESTED CENTERS FOR CHOCOLATES

Plain fondant mixed with chopped nuts or fruit
Butter cream mixed with chopped nuts
Maple creams
Oriental creams
Nougats
Caramels
Butter crunch

Butter brickal
Toffee
Cherries dipped first in fondant
Fruits
Jellies
Apricot paste
Apricot orange balls
Marzipan

HAZELNUT TRUFFLES

1 cup hazelnuts (finely grated)
½ cup sugar
2 squares grated bitter chocolate (2 ounces)

½ cup water
2 tablespoons confectioners' sugar
2 teaspoons cocoa

Mix 1 cup finely grated hazelnuts with ½ cup sugar and 2 squares grated chocolate in a 1-quart saucepan. Blend in ½ cup water gradually. Put over low heat, stirring constantly until chocolate is melted and sugar dissolved. The mixture will be thick and hard to handle. Cool, then form into balls and roll in a mixture of 2 tablespoons confectioners' sugar and 2 teaspoons cocoa.

HAZELNUT TRUFFLES WITH SEMISWEET CHOCOLATE

1 cup toasted hazelnuts (finely grated)
1 cup confectioners' sugar
1 egg white
2 packages semisweet chocolate (12 ounces)
¼ cup cream

Grate 1 cup toasted hazelnuts and blend with 1 cup confectioners' sugar. Add just enough egg white to make a firm paste. Melt 2 packages semisweet chocolate over hot water. Scald ¼ cup cream and cool to temperature of chocolate. Pour cream into chocolate and mix with a wooden spoon until blended, then mix in hazelnut paste. Put into a pan lined with waxed paper and set in a cool place. Cut in oblongs or squares when hard. Or form into balls and roll in cocoa or chocolate shot.

FRENCH CHOCOLATES

1 pound sweet dark or milk chocolate
⅓ cup heavy cream
½ cup finely grated toasted nuts (optional)

Winter Holidays

Melt 1 pound sweet dark or milk chocolate slowly over hot water. Scald ⅓ cup heavy cream and let cool down to the same temperature as the chocolate. Pour the cream into the chocolate and beat quickly with wooden spoon until thoroughly mixed. Pat into a pan lined with waxed paper and slice off in oblong shapes when set. For variety add ½ cup grated toasted nuts after beating in the cream.

CHOCOLATE PRALINES

1 cup sugar
1 cup nuts — almonds or hazelnuts

½ pound sweet or semisweet dipping chocolate

Measure 1 cup sugar and 1 cup nuts into a heavy skillet and cook over medium heat, stirring occasionally until sugar melts and nuts begin to make popping sounds. Pour into greased pan. Let cool and then grind finely and mix with ½ pound melted chocolate. Pour into a pan (8 by 11 inches) which has been lined with waxed paper and mark in squares. When cool cut and serve plain or dipped in chocolate.

CHOCOLATE CREAMS

6 one-ounce semisweet chocolate pieces
1 tablespoon butter

½ cup sweetened condensed milk
¾ teaspoon vanilla

Melt 6 ounces chocolate and 1 tablespoon butter in a double boiler. Add ½ cup sweetened condensed milk and cook until thick. Then add ¾ teaspoon vanilla. This will take about 15 minutes of cooking, until the candy is thick enough to drop by spoonfuls and hold its shape. It may be shaped into centers and dipped in chocolate or fondant.

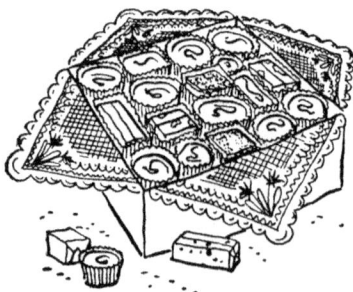

Spring Holidays

FOR the candymaker Easter is the big spring-time challenge. Candy eggs of one sort or another are the Easter specialties, along with marshmallow chicks and chocolate bunnies. But here again those friends of yours who have been going without sweets for Lent will welcome your best candies whatever shape they come in. If you are not an expert yet, this is the time to try your hand at fudge or its near relatives, penuche and pralines.

But once you have mastered chocolate dipping you will not want to miss the fun of making chocolate-coated Easter eggs big enough to decorate with pink or yellow flowers, green leaves and a bright name written across the top.

If you can find molds in bunny shapes in your neighborhood, Easter bunnies are also fun to make, either out of marshmallow, to be dipped in chocolate, or out of solid chocolate. Dust the molds with cornstarch and spoon in the marshmallow as soon as it has reached the right consistency for pouring. Chill and then dip in chocolate. Or melt semisweet or milk chocolate and pour into the molds.

Chicks can be shaped with scissors from cooled marshmallow, and then dipped in yellow colored sugar. Use pieces of nut for the eye and the bill.

For an Easter Saturday variation from coloring and painting real eggs, let the children in on the decorating of their own chocolate eggs or even on making marshmallow chicks.

Candy is welcomed on St. Patrick's Day because it is a break in the Lenten fast and because the green-colored candies are everyone's favorite. Make pulled mints, green mint patties decorated with shamrocks, and green jellied candies or hard candies in shamrock shapes.

On April Fool's Day do not leave the field to the practical joker who presents you with chocolate-covered soap or pepper-flavored bonbons. There is an older tradition which calls for real candy, made in clown colors of red, green and white for presentation on the first day of April. Nougats made with red cherries and green pistachio nuts are just right for the occasion. So is divinity with the same mixture.

Welcome spring on May Day with spun sugar

molded into little May baskets which can be filled with tiny crystallized fondant flowers.

Spun-sugar nests can also be used for Easter and for decorating special ice-cream desserts. If you undertake spun sugar you will need a big cleared space in your kitchen. You'll have a gay time spinning it, and the delicate gossamer threads which result are well worth the time and effort of the after-job of cleaning up.

EASTER EGGS

Easter eggs may be made either from marshmallow, divinity or butter creams. Butter creams are prefer-

able to plain fondant. Except for miniature eggs, Oriental creams are too runny to use at all. Very large eggs must be dipped a second time after the first coating has hardened so that the filling will not ooze. Marshmallow eggs may be shaped by hand before the mixture is cold or may be cut into shape with scissors. For decorating use royal icing tinted pink, yellow and green. Use a small pastry tube. With a little practice you will be able to make rosettes and write names with the best of them. Outlines of bunnies or large flowers may be used instead of names.

SPUN SUGAR

2 cups sugar	1 cup water
1 teaspoon light corn syrup	⅛ teaspoon cream of tartar

Measure 2 cups sugar, 1 teaspoon light corn syrup and 1 cup water in a saucepan and blend together. Place over low heat and stir until mixture boils, then add ⅛ teaspoon cream of tartar. Wash down sides of pan with pastry brush or fork wrapped with muslin (dipped in water) to prevent crystal formation on the pan. Put in the candy thermometer and continue to boil without stirring until the thermometer registers 310°. The candy at this stage forms fine threads very readily. Dip a warm spoon in the hot syrup and shake back and forth over a long metal candy bar that has been greased. Many threads will form which may be gathered up and shaped as you wish. It takes practice to move the spoon fast enough to form the threads and not let drops of syrup fall. Just the right amount of syrup must be on the spoon to form the threads as the spoon is moved back and forth. Spun sugar has no keeping qualities and must be used almost immediately. It may be formed into nests to be used for Easter baskets or it may be used to decorate special ice-cream desserts.

PULLED MINTS

2 cups sugar	1 tablespoon light corn syrup
⅔ cup water	Flavor and coloring

Measure 2 cups sugar, ⅔ cup water and 1 tablespoon light corn syrup into a 2-quart saucepan and blend well. Place over low heat and stir until sugar dissolves and mixture comes to a boil. Wash away any crystals that may form while cooking, using either a pastry brush or a fork wrapped in muslin and dipped in water. Put in thermometer after syrup boils and cook without stirring until 265° is reached. Remove from heat and pour candy onto buttered plates, dividing into portions to be colored separately. When the candy is cool enough to handle fold edges in to the center. Keep other portions warm in a slow oven while the first portion is pulled. Add flavor and coloring as you start pulling – 1 teaspoon peppermint extract is enough for the whole batch – the amount of coloring depends on the tint desired. Pull the candy, using cornstarch on the hands to prevent sticking. When the candy is hard to pull and has become quite cool, twist it out into a long rope and cut into small pieces. Dust each piece with confectioners' sugar and store in an airtight container. After a few days the candy will become smooth and mellow. Pink, green and white are the usual colors, with peppermint the favorite flavor.

DIVINITY AND NOUGATS

Divinity, sea foam, its brown-sugar variation, and nougat all belong to the same general family of candies made with an egg-white base, though nougat varies quite distinctly from the others in both flavor and texture.

But the secret of making both candies lies in just two things: bringing the syrup up to the right temperature and beating the mixture long enough. Both of these candies really require an electric beater.

Divinity has been made by every high school girl with the same fervor with which she makes chocolate fudge, and indeed good divinity tastes and looks more like white fudge than vanilla fudge does.

But somehow or other, despite the popularity of nougat as a commercial candy, few people attempt to make it at home. This is partly because most recipes are of the type that demand nougat paper to spread over the top and bottom of the candy, and nougat paper is hard to get, although fish-food wafers may be substituted. Also, most recipes for nougat produce a sticky, runny candy that will not hold up and is hardly likely to be tried a second time.

Both the nougat recipes presented here have a slightly chewy texture, and if divinity can be called white fudge, then these nougats could be called white caramels. This chewy quality comes with the addition of butter to the recipe and helps ensure a piece of candy that will hold its shape. The two part, three step process is much less difficult than it seems and is important because the second syrup can be added at a much higher temperature, when the egg whites have already been whipped up with a small amount of honey or syrup cooked to a lower temperature. We have found this type of nougat so much more success-ful for the home kitchen that it is the only type we present.

DIVINITY

2 cups sugar	Dash of salt
½ cup corn syrup	¾ teaspoon vanilla
½ cup water	1 cup nuts, chopped (op-
2 egg whites (¼ cup)	tional)

Combine 2 cups sugar with ½ cup corn syrup and ½ cup water. Stir over low heat until all the sugar is dissolved, and let this mixture boil over medium heat to 256°. Remove from the heat and let stand while 2 egg whites (¼ cup) are beaten to stiff peaks. A dash of salt is added to the egg whites while beating them. Slowly add the syrup to the egg whites, beating continuously. After all the syrup is added continue beating until candy holds a definite shape and no longer streams from a spoon. This will require at least 15 minutes of beating and an electric mixer will make the job easier. A test can be made before the beating is stopped and unless the dropped portion holds its shape immediately, beating should be continued. When it is ready ¾ teaspoon vanilla is quickly stirred in, along with nuts, and then the candy is dropped on waxed paper in teaspoon-size pieces. It may also be poured into a pan (8 by 11 inches) and cut into squares. Black walnuts, pecans and toasted hazelnuts are excellent choices for this confection.

Spring Holidays

SEA FOAM

3 cups light brown sugar	2 egg whites (¼ cup)
¾ cup water	Dash of salt
1 tablespoon light corn syrup	1 teaspoon vanilla extract

Measure 3 cups light brown sugar, ¾ cup water and one tablespoon light corn syrup into a 2-quart saucepan. Blend with a wooden spoon, and place over low heat, stirring continuously until the mixture begins to dissolve. Continue stirring until the mixture boils, then put in your candy thermometer and boil without stirring over medium-high heat until the thermometer registers 256°. Remove from heat and let stand while 2 egg whites (¼ cup) are beaten to stiff peaks. A dash of salt is added to the eggs while beating them. Slowly add the syrup to the egg whites, beating continuously. After all the syrup is added continue beating until candy holds a definite shape and no longer streams from a spoon and loses its gloss. This will require at least 15 minutes of beating and an electric mixer will make the job easier. A test can be made before the beating is stopped and unless the dropped portion holds its shape immediately, beating should be continued. One teaspoon vanilla is stirred in just before candy is dropped in teaspoon-size pieces on waxed paper. Walnuts or pecans may be added — they combine well with brown-sugar candies.

NOUGAT

First Part

¾ cup sugar
2 tablespoons water
⅔ cup light corn syrup

¼ cup egg whites at room temperature

Second Part

2 cups sugar
2 cups light corn syrup
¼ cup butter

2 teaspoons vanilla
2 cups toasted whole almonds

½ cup pistachio nuts

For the first part, measure ¾ cup sugar, 2 tablespoons water and ⅔ cup light corn syrup into a 1-quart saucepan. Blend with a wooden spoon and place over low heat, stirring continuously until the mixture begins to dissolve. Continue stirring until the mixture boils, then put in your candy thermometer and boil without stirring over medium-high heat until the thermometer registers 238°. Remove from the heat and let stand while beating ¼ cup egg whites, which are at room temperature, to stiff peaks. Slowly add the hot syrup to the beaten egg whites, beating continuously, and continue to beat until thick and somewhat cool. This should require at least 5 minutes of beating with an electric beater. Let the mixture stand.

For the second part, measure 2 cups sugar and 2 cups light corn syrup in a 2-quart saucepan. Blend with a wooden spoon, and place over low heat, stirring continuously until the mixture begins to dissolve. Continue stirring until the mixture boils, then put in your candy thermometer and boil without stirring over medium-high heat until the thermometer registers 280°. Let this syrup stand until it stops bubbling, then pour it all into the first mixture and beat with a wooden spoon vigorously until both mixtures are well combined. Add the ¼ cup butter in small pieces and continue beating until very thick. Two teaspoons vanilla, and 2 cups toasted almonds and ½ cup pistachio nuts are added at the last and the whole mixture stirred well to get an even distribution of nutmeats. Pour into two pans, 8 by 8 inches, and allow to remain overnight in a cool place before cutting. Cut into pieces and wrap in individual papers. Candied cherries may also be added at the same time as the nutmeats.

HONEY NOUGAT

2 cups sugar	5 tablespoons **honey**
2 cups corn syrup	¼ cup butter
½ cup water	½ teaspoon vanilla
¼ cup egg whites	1 cup toasted almonds

Measure 2 cups sugar, 2 cups corn syrup and ½ cup water into a 2-quart saucepan. Blend with a wooden spoon and place over low heat, stirring continuously until the mixture begins to dissolve. Continue stirring

until it boils, then put in your candy thermometer and boil without stirring over medium-high heat until the thermometer registers 300°. Meanwhile beat ¼ cup egg whites to a stiff peak and slowly add 5 tablespoons honey. Remove mixture from heat and let stand until it stops bubbling. Then add the hot syrup to the egg whites and honey, beating continuously.

Add ¼ cup butter which has been broken into small pieces and beat in well. When very thick add ½ teaspoon vanilla and 1 cup almonds which have been well toasted, pour into a pan, 8 by 11 inches, and let stand overnight in a cool place. Cut with a heavy knife and wrap in waxed paper or moistureproof cellophane. This is an excellent nougat for coating with chocolate. The honey content keeps it soft and tender.

FUDGE

Fudge and fondant are close relatives. Both are cooked to the same temperature range, 234° to 240°. And neither is beaten until it has cooled, to gain a creamy fine-grained texture. If you wish, you can even treat fudge just as though it were fondant and pour it onto a slab or tray, working it with a paddle or spatula instead of beating with a spoon. This is a speedier process because the candy cools more quickly when it is spread out than it does when left to cool in the pan.

If you like fudge with a soft creamy texture, you may want to try working it this way, although the texture will be just about as smooth if you cool your candy long enough before beating it in the pan.

The best temperature for beating creamy fudge is the same as that for fondant, about 110°, when the candy feels warm under your fingers but not uncomfortably warm. If you cool it in the pan you can leave the thermometer in and wait until it comes down to the exact degree.

To discover the proper temperature for beating fudge to give it the hardness and slight grain that many prefer, we left the thermometer in several batches and beat each at a different temperature. We discovered that if the fudge is beaten much higher than 150° it will become sugary — a condition that seems to be liked only in New Orleans pralines. But at 150° it seems to acquire just the hardness and texture that belongs to the best of old-fashioned home-made fudge.

Of course, the corn syrup in the fudge recipes acts as a brake against complete sugaring. Brown sugar has its own "brake," so in those recipes using it, corn syrup is not needed.

We have included pralines in with the fudges, although one recipe is cooked to a slightly higher degree, because they are more like a sugary fudge than they are like any other candy.

Most candies of the general fudge classification, because they are so sweet tasting, improve with the addition of nuts, raisins, if you like, or cut bits of marshmallow.

Fudge keeps well only if wrapped in waxed paper or put in a tin box, and even then will harden or sugar with age. So if you are making fudge for gift boxes make it toward the end of your schedule.

CHOCOLATE FUDGE

2 cups sugar	2 squares baking chocolate
1/3 cup corn syrup	1 tablespoon butter
2/3 cup milk or equal parts milk and cream	1 teaspoon vanilla

Measure 2 cups sugar, 1/3 cup corn syrup and 2/3 cup milk or equal parts milk and cream (for a richer fudge) into a 3-quart saucepan. Blend and add 2 squares baking chocolate. Place over low heat and stir carefully until chocolate is melted and sugar dissolved. Continue stirring until mixture begins to boil, then put in your thermometer and cook over medium heat, stirring only if candy sticks, until the temperature reaches 238°. Remove from stove, add 1 tablespoon butter but do not stir. Keep the thermometer in the pan and if you want an old-fashioned hard fudge start beating when the temperature goes down to

150°. Remove thermometer, add 1 teaspoon vanilla and beat until the candy begins to lose its gloss, turns lighter in color and begins to feel a little grainy under your spoon. Turn out into a buttered pan, 8 by 8 inches, and mark into squares. For a creamy fudge, wait until the temperature goes down to 110°, then

add vanilla and beat until thick and creamy. This may take as long as 15 minutes depending on the humidity and this fudge will become much lighter than that beaten at the higher temperature. It will not really "fudge" at all but be more the consistency of fondant. You can pour it out onto a marble slab or platter and work it like fondant if you prefer.

Spring Holidays

OPERA FUDGE or VANILLA FUDGE

2 cups sugar	½ cup milk
1 cup heavy cream	¼ cup corn syrup
1 teaspoon vanilla	

Measure 2 cups sugar, 1 cup heavy cream, ½ cup milk and ¼ cup corn syrup into a 3-quart saucepan and stir over low heat until sugar is dissolved. Continue stirring until it boils, put in your thermometer and boil over medium heat until the temperature reaches 238°. Cool to 110°, add 1 teaspoon vanilla and beat until thick and creamy. For a harder fudge, begin beating when it has cooled only to 150°. This fudge is known by many names including Opera Caramels and Chantilly Fudge.

PENUCHE

1 pound brown sugar (2⅓ cups)	2 tablespoons butter
¾ cup milk or equal parts milk and cream	1 teaspoon vanilla

Measure 1 pound brown sugar and ¾ cup milk or milk and cream into a 3-quart saucepan and stir over low heat until the sugar dissolves. Continue stirring until it boils, then put in your candy thermometer and boil over medium heat until it reaches a temperature

The Holiday Candy Book

of 237°. Remove from heat and add 2 tablespoons butter but do not stir. For a creamy penuche, cool to 110°, add 1 teaspoon vanilla and beat until thick and creamy. Turn into a buttered pan, 8 by 8 inches. For a harder, more sugary candy, let cool to 150° and beat until the candy begins to lose its gloss and begins to feel a little grainy under the spoon. Penuche is easier to doctor than chocolate fudge, if you miss the perfect moment for turning it out. If it becomes too hard, you can thin it with a small amount of cream, which will lessen the grainy texture, too.

NEW ORLEANS PRALINES I

2 cups sugar	1 cup hot water
1 cup light brown sugar	2 cups whole small pecans

Mix 2 cups sugar, 1 cup light brown sugar and 1 cup hot water in a 3-quart saucepan and blend and stir over low heat until sugar dissolves. Add 2 cups whole pecans, continue stirring until mixture boils. Put in your thermometer and boil over medium heat, stirring only occasionally until temperature reaches 236°. Remove from heat and begin to beat immediately with a wooden spoon. Beat only about 5 minutes until candy begins to lose its gloss and appears only slightly granular. Pour into greased muffin pans as thinly as possible. If the mixture begins to thicken too much, reheat over hot water. This is a very sugary type of brown-sugar fudge with the full flavor of the syrup saturating the pecans because they are cooked right in it. It's good and sweet.

NEW ORLEANS PRALINES II (*with butter*)

2 cups light brown sugar	¼ cup butter
¼ cup water	2 cups small pecan meats

Measure 2 cups light brown sugar, ¼ cup water and ¼ cup butter into a 2-quart saucepan and stir over low heat until sugar dissolves and mixture boils. Put in thermometer and add nutmeats. Boil slowly, stirring constantly until temperature reaches 248°. Remove from heat and immediately drop by tablespoons on waxed paper or into greased muffin or patty pans. This is a richer praline than the first recipe, less creamy in texture and less opaque.

Summer Holidays

JUNE weddings and their anniversaries usher in the summer candy season. One wedding anniversary — the sixth — is dedicated to sugar and candy — and to iron, too. But candy is wonderful for any wedding celebration. Because of their fresh dainty look, pastel and white bonbons are wedding party specials along with white mints and the ever-present fondant patty. For weddings or anniversaries the patty is left white and flavored to your taste, then decorated with flowers of royal icing put on with a pastry tube. Patties can be made large enough so that names may be written on them, and they can be used for place cards at any party or celebration.

Summertime is really not the perfect time to make candy — let's face it. But you can do a good job with most varieties if you pick the less humid days.

Marshmallows are no problem and they are just right for a Fourth of July picnic, either eaten with the fingers or toasted on sticks. Jellied candies appear cool

and are refreshing; so they are well liked in warm
weather even though they are more difficult to make.
This is so with hard candies as well. And I might as
well say that there are no licorice candies in this book
because of the many difficulties in the way of han-
dling licorice in the home kitchen. Most professional

anise

candymakers don't make their own licorice candies
but buy them from specialists in the field. Partly this
is because licorice candy traditionally must be colored
black, which involves using chemicals. The licorice
root itself is not black but somewhere back in unre-
corded history it was used in black candy and the
idea caught on. So it isn't licorice if it isn't black. If

you like the flavor you can get a good approximation
by using anise – only then, according to tradition,
you must color it red, or it isn't anise!

If you stir up some butter crunch, everybody's favorite, you will not need to worry about how it keeps.
It will disappear so quickly the weather will not have
a chance to affect it. And the same is true of peanut

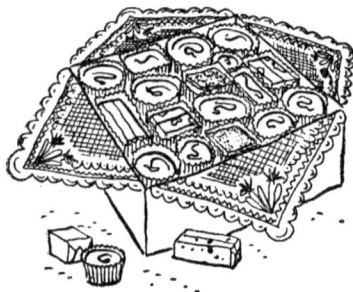

brittle, a favorite summertime confection which is apt
to get sticky if left around. But do not attempt to dip
chocolates in hot weather unless you have air con-
ditioning.

Mother's Day and Father's Day come before it gets
really hot so you need not be too limited in your
choice of candies to make for either parent's day. Gift
boxes at this time, like those for birthdays or presentation at any season of the year, deserve a special job

of packing. You can arrange candies in pretty dishes and wrap them in cellophane. Nuts and small hard candies look attractive packed in marmalade jars. If your assortment includes chocolates they will look best packed in a pretty tin box or in a pasteboard box lined with lace paper. You can use doilies or shelf edging.

To pack a box fit cardboard separators to the proper size so that the layers will sit evenly. Put your heaviest pieces in the bottom and save the most decorative for the top layer. If you can get small glassine candy cups it will help to keep your candy looking nice and make it easier to arrange. They are difficult to find nowadays, though.

If the candy is to be shipped, pack it tightly so there isn't room for it to slide around and become marred or broken. Put cellophane over the top layer and crush waxed paper under the lid of the box. Then wrap it all in corrugated paper and mark it "perishable."

For Fourth of July stay-at-homes fondant patties turn up again, this time in oblong shapes, decorated with red stripes and blue stars to simulate flags. For table decorations, too, which the young guests can lick at later, make red and white candy sticks, wrap

them in red cellophane and twist the ends to make
firecrackers.

MARSHMALLOWS AND JELLIES

Marshmallows are just about the most satisfying
candy you can turn your hand to. They are melting,
delicate, luscious — a taste and texture revelation —
and so much better than the commercial product that
there is hardly a basis for comparison. Made of nothing but sugar syrup, gelatin and flavoring they are
also one of the most inexpensive candies to make. You
really do need an electric mixer for the beating process, though, because it takes strong, regular and pro-
longed beating to achieve a marshmallow.

Its close relatives, jellies or Turkish paste — though
you wouldn't believe it to look at them — are more
difficult to make at home, as the best jellied candies
include a large amount of cornstarch, which is difficult to cook to the right stage without scorching.
Commercially, jellied candies are made in steam-
jacketed kettles to prevent this. Also, it is difficult to
find flavors good enough to "stand alone" — as the
flavors in jellied candies must, since there is no flavor
added by cream or butter or other such ingredients.

Summer Holidays

The two recipes given here are the result of long experimentation. The gelatin recipe is the most delicate in texture. But we feel that the Jello recipe made with cornstarch is a real discovery for home cooks, since it uses the variety of concentrated flavors that have been developed for dessert use, with the addition of enough cornstarch to give a slightly chewy texture.

We have also included in this chapter some natural fruit jellies. These are not clear jellies and are used chiefly for centers for dipping in fondant or chocolate (see pages 19–28 and 32–37).

MARSHMALLOWS

2 tablespoons gelatin	¾ cup light corn syrup
(2 envelopes)	½ cup hot water
½ cup cold water	2 teaspoons vanilla
2 cups sugar	Confectioners' sugar

Put 2 tablespoons gelatin in an electric mixer bowl and measure into this ½ cup cold water. Mix well and let stand. Measure 2 cups sugar, ¾ cup light corn syrup and ½ cup hot water into a saucepan and blend well with a wooden spoon. Place over low heat until sugar is all dissolved and then increase the heat. When mixture boils put in your candy thermometer and continue cooking without stirring. When thermometer registers 244° to 246°, remove from heat and pour into gelatin, beating all the while. Continue beating until candy thickens and is slightly warm. At least 15 minutes is required. Blend in 2 teaspoons vanilla and pour into two pans (7 by 7 inches) that have been lightly buttered and dusted with cornstarch. Set in a cool place or refrigerator until firm. Remove from pan and cut into pieces, dusting each piece well with confectioners' sugar. Scissors can be used if dipped in confectioners' sugar between cuttings. Marshmallow can be dipped in chocolate, or combined with equal-size pieces of caramel or jellies for dipping. Or marshmallow may be used between two layers of caramel to give a variation.

A drop of fruit coloring may be added to the mixture during the beating to give tinted marshmallows. Concentrated canned or frozen fruit juice or strong coffee may be used in place of the cold water in which the gelatin is soaked. In this case, omit the vanilla. For nut marshmallows add ½ cup chopped nuts to the mixture, or roll the marshmallow pieces in finely chopped nuts.

GELATIN JELLIES

2 tablespoons gelatin (2 envelopes)	Juice and grated rind of 1 lemon
½ cup cold water	Juice and grated rind of 1 eating orange
2 cups sugar	Granulated or confectioners' sugar
½ cup hot water	

Soften 2 tablespoons gelatin in ½ cup cold water and let stand. Measure 2 cups sugar and ½ cup hot water into a 2- or 3-quart saucepan, stirring over low heat until it dissolves and begins to boil. Now put in your thermometer and boil over high heat until the temperature reaches 290°. Add the gelatin to this syrup and cook slowly over low heat until the thermometer registers 228°. Strain juice and grated rind of 1 orange and 1 lemon into the mixture, blend and pour into an 8-inch square pan which has been rinsed in cold water and not dried. Chill in the refrigerator until set and firm. Remove and let stand in a cool room for an hour or two. Remove from the pan and cut into cubes. Roll in either granulated or confectioners' sugar. Let stand another hour before packing into a tin box. These do not keep well over a long period and are a little softer than commercial jellies or Turkish paste.

JELLO JELLIES

1 cup sugar	1 package desired flavor
3 tablespoons cornstarch	Jello
1 cup boiling water	¼ cup boiling water

Mix 1 cup sugar and 3 tablespoons cornstarch together in a 2-quart saucepan and add 1 cup boiling water. Blend well and place over low heat, stirring

cherries

raspberries

constantly until the mixture is clear. Then add 1 package Jello which has been mixed with ¼ cup boiling water. Put in the candy thermometer and stir until thermometer registers 222°. Remove from heat and let stand until cool. Spoon out in patty shapes on greased cookie sheets. Let stand until firm and either roll in granulated sugar or dip in chocolate. Jello comes in strawberry, raspberry, lemon, lime, cherry and orange flavors.

Summer Holidays

APRICOT JELLY

1 pound dried apricots   2 cups sugar

Steam 1 pound dried apricots until very soft. Put through a baby-food strainer into a saucepan. Measure 2 cups sugar into the strained apricots and slowly cook over low heat until mixture forms a very heavy string from the end of the spoon. This candy must be stirred continuously to keep it from scorching. It is difficult to use a thermometer for this thick candy. However, a test in cold water may be made. When the candy holds its shape and is quite thick, remove from heat. It may be spooned out into patties on a lightly greased platter or large pan or poured into a pan and later cut into cubes. Patties or cubes may be dipped in chocolate or fondant, or they are good just rolled in sugar.

PINEAPPLE JELLY

2 cups sugar
1/2 cup water
1 cup grated pineapple, drained
2 envelopes gelatin ⎫
 (2 tablespoons)   ⎬ mix and let stand at least
1/4 cup cold water ⎭   5 minutes

Measure 2 cups sugar and 1/2 cup water into a saucepan and blend well together. Place over low heat and stir until all the sugar is dissolved. When it boils, put in the candy thermometer and increase the heat. When the thermometer registers 254° measure in 1 cup drained grated pineapple, stir and continue

pineapple

cooking until candy becomes thick and jellied. Remove from the heat and add 2 envelopes gelatin which has been softened in ¼ cup cold water. Pour into a lightly greased pan and set in a cool place overnight before cutting. This is especially good dipped in chocolate or fondant. The pieces may be squares or caramel size.

HARD CANDIES, CRUNCHES AND BRITTLES

Hard candies are a good change from the sweet, soft or chewy fudges, caramels and marshmallows. Clear hard candies are cooked to just about the top of the candy thermometer's range — as high as 310° —

and form the basis for lollipops, drops, barley-sugar twists and so on. This candy is hard enough to merit the name "jawbreaker" and is relished most by the very young and the very old.

But there are other candies cooked to slightly lower temperatures — the toffees, brittles and crunches — which are more tender on the teeth because of the addition of butter. Of all these, probably butter crunch is in highest favor right now, particularly when coated with chocolate and nuts. This is one of the quickest, easiest candies to cook with the right utensils, though it is also one of the most expensive since it is made of equal quantities of butter and sugar. Butter brickal is a variation which contains a good deal less butter.

Brittles are usually poured out as thin as possible and stretched after pouring when the edges begin to cool to make a very thin, brittle and tender candy to eat. The addition of the butter and nuts 20° under the temperature at which the candy is finished ensures a good brown taste to both nuts and brittle and makes it easier to work the butter in without stirring the candy so much that it sugars. The addition of soda, traditional with peanut brittle, makes the candy less transparent and imparts a special texture as well.

Toffee is really a simple caramel cooked to a temperature which makes it hard instead of chewy. The recipe we give is one we used incessantly one summer we spent at a lake along with one of our aunts. We made it after we got home, too, but never could find the recipe or remember the exact measurements, simple though they are, and always had to call Aunt Ann to get the proportions again. Someone finally wrote it into Mother's special recipe book and we made it again and still found it good.

BASIC HARD CANDY

2 cups sugar	¾ cup water
⅔ cup light corn syrup	Flavorings and colorings

Measure 2 cups sugar, ⅔ cup light corn syrup and ¾ cup water into a saucepan and blend together. Place over low heat and stir until mixture boils. Cover the saucepan for 5 minutes so that any sugar crystals that have formed on the sides of the pan will be washed down. Now put in the candy thermometer and let the candy boil without stirring. Using a pastry brush or a fork wrapped with muslin and dipped in water, wash off any crystals that might form. After the candy reaches 280°, lower heat so as not to discolor the candy. When candy thermometer registers 300°, remove pan from the heat and allow it to stand until all the bubbles have simmered down. Then add the flavoring and coloring. There are many to choose from but one favorite is anise along with red coloring. One teaspoon of a flavoring extract should be used for this recipe, while only a few drops of an oil such as peppermint, wintergreen or cinnamon are enough. Coloring should be added gradually until the desired intensity is reached. It is important to stir these in as gently as possible. Too much stirring will cause the syrup to solidify into a hard sugary lump. Now the candy is ready to be formed. It may be poured into a pan, 7 by 7 inches, and marked into squares as it begins to harden. Or it may be poured in rounds on skewers or sticks to form lollipops.

BUTTER CRUNCH

¾ pound butter	1 cup grated nuts
¾ pound sugar (1½ cups)	½ pound dipping chocolate
1 teaspoon corn syrup	*or* 6 ounces semisweet
½ cup chopped nuts	chocolate

Melt ¾ pound butter in a 10-inch heavy iron skillet, add 1½ cups sugar and 1 teaspoon corn syrup and, stirring constantly, bring to a boil. Put in your thermometer, which will have to be put in at a slant or held with one hand while you stir with the other. Continue stirring over medium heat until the temperature reaches 290°. Remove from heat, stir in ½ cup chopped nuts and pour into a large flat pan or tray. The sugar and butter will not blend well until they reach about 250°. But they should not separate after that if you keep the temperature high enough to keep the mixture bubbling.

When the mixture has cooled, melt the chocolate (you may use more or less depending on the thickness you prefer) and spread thinly over surface, then sprinkle with half of the cup of grated nuts. When the chocolate hardens, turn the candy over and cover the other side with melted chocolate and the remaining nuts.

You may coat only one side with chocolate and nuts if you wish. A quick way of putting chocolate on both sides is to spread the pan you are going to use with grated nuts, smooth melted chocolate over them and then pour your candy onto this layer. As soon as candy cools slightly, spread pieces of chocolate over it with a spatula, letting the warm candy melt the top layer of chocolate; then sprinkle with nuts.

PEANUT BRITTLE

1½ cups sugar	1 tablespoon butter
1 cup light corn syrup	1½ cups salted peanuts
⅓ cup water	1 teaspoon baking soda
½ teaspoon vanilla	

Measure 1½ cups sugar, 1 cup light corn syrup and ⅓ cup water into a 3-quart saucepan and stir over low heat until sugar dissolves. Continue stirring until syrup boils, then put in your thermometer and boil over high heat until thermometer registers 280°. Lower heat and add 1 tablespoon butter, stirring rapidly, then 1½ cups salted peanuts. If your peanuts are not salted add ½ teaspoon salt. Cook and stir for 2 or 3 minutes, then stir occasionally until temperature reaches 300°. Remove from heat, add 1 teaspoon soda (which should be free from lumps) and stir until it bubbles up, add ½ teaspoon vanilla, stir again and then pour onto two large cookie sheets. Spread out thinly with a spatula and when the edges are cool enough to handle pick them up and stretch out as thinly as possible. As the candy cools down pull it loose from the pan and turn it over, stretching again. This candy does not keep well and will get sticky unless kept in a tightly covered tin.

BUTTERSCOTCH

1½ cups white sugar	⅔ cup cold water
½ cup light brown sugar	½ cup butter
½ cup light corn syrup	¼ teaspoon salt

Measure 1½ cups white sugar, ½ cup light brown sugar, ½ cup light corn syrup, and ⅔ cup cold water in a saucepan. Place over low heat and stir well until mixture boils. Cover the pan for 5 minutes so that the steam will wash down any sugar crystals on the sides of the pan. Remove cover and put in the candy thermometer and let boil without stirring until thermometer registers 280°. Now add ½ cup butter and ¼ teaspoon salt and continue cooking until the thermometer registers 310°. Pour into a large greased pan, 13 by 9 inches, and mark into squares when the butterscotch begins to set. For patties, molds may be used or, if you have a steady hand, you can shape them by hand or else use a funnel and stick, only be sure to oil and heat both the funnel and the stick.

BUTTER BRICKAL

1¼ cups butter	½ cup water
2½ cups sugar	1 teaspoon salt
1 cup chopped nuts	

Measure 1¼ cups butter and 2½ cups sugar into a heavy 2- or 3-quart saucepan, add ½ cup water and 1 teaspoon salt and place over low heat, stirring until dissolved. When the mixture boils add 1 cup chopped nuts. Put in your thermometer and boil until 290° is reached, stirring occasionally toward the end. Pour into a large pan or tray. Mark in squares and cut or break when cold. Wrap in waxed paper or cellophane. This may be covered with chocolate and nuts like butter crunch, or the squares may be dipped in chocolate.

MAPLE–NUT BRITTLE

⅓ cup white sugar	⅓ cup water
⅔ cup maple syrup	1 cup nuts
¾ cup light corn syrup	2 tablespoons butter
⅛ teaspoon salt	

Measure ⅓ cup white sugar, ⅔ cup maple syrup, ¾ cup light corn syrup and ⅓ cup water into a

black walnut

saucepan and blend together. Place over low heat and stir until mixture boils. Wash crystals from sides of pan using either a pastry brush or a muslin wrapped fork that has been dipped in water. Now put in the candy thermometer and boil without stirring until the thermometer registers 280°. At this point, put in 1 cup nuts, 2 tablespoons butter and ⅛ teaspoon salt. Continue cooking until thermometer registers 305°. Pour out on a large pan and, when cool enough to handle, stretch the candy out as thin as possible.

TOFFEE

2 cups sugar	1 teaspoon of either vanilla
2 cups dark corn syrup	or rum flavoring
⅓ cup butter	

Measure 2 cups sugar, 2 cups dark corn syrup and ⅓ cup butter into a saucepan and blend together. Place over low heat and stir until mixture boils. Now put in your candy thermometer and allow to boil without stirring until thermometer reaches 270°. Remove from heat and add flavoring. Pour into a pan, 7 by 11 inches, and mark into squares or rectangles before the candy hardens. Wrap each piece in waxed paper or moistureproof cellophane.

Autumn Holidays

DARKNESS comes earlier; the reluctant schol-
ars are scurrying off to school again; the
harvest moon is on its way and Halloween
is about to raise its ghosts. Fall has arrived and the
children have taken over the candy kitchen.

For this is the season of the year that is their own
special time, the season of candy apples on a stick,
of taffy pulls and popcorn balls, of Halloween faces
on orange lollipops and the whole Thanksgiving
repertoire of fruit and nut confections.

This is the time of year when you let the children
try their skill at caramels after school, when candymaking can become the chief function at a children's
party, when something sweet is just what is needed
to allay that hungry feeling still there even at the
end of a good trencherman's meal.

And this is the time when you pack those big boxes
of luscious goodies to send off to the older ones away
at school — and they must be big boxes so your own

youngster can have a chance for at least a piece when all his friends and roommates come crowding in for a treat.

The holidays of fall are Halloween and Thanksgiving and each has its special candies, but fall is a continuous candy holiday for children.

FRUIT AND NUT CONFECTIONS

Because they are usually less sweet, fruit and nut candies are favored by many as the finishing touch

lemon

of a Thanksgiving or other holiday meal when the food has already been rich and ample. But they disappear rapidly no matter how solid the meal, so make plenty while you are doing it. Most of these candies are easy to make. Except for glacéed nuts they keep well over a longer period than do most candies.

Apricots, prunes and dates are the most favored fruits, along with citrus peel, and there are innumerable variations in the way they are treated. We include the simplest as well as the best of the methods we tried.

Any nut you like may be used in candymaking and most nuts are a welcome addition to such candies as fudge, nougat, divinity and caramels. Here they stand on their own with just a touch of sweetness added.

APRICOT COCONUT BALLS

1 cup dried apricots	1 teaspoon grated lemon
1 cup dry coconut	rind
¾ cup nuts — almonds,	1 teaspoon lemon juice
pecans or walnuts	1 tablespoon orange juice

2 tablespoons confectioners' sugar or more

Steam 1 cup dried apricots in the top of a double boiler for 10 minutes, then grind with 1 cup coconut and ¾ cup nuts, putting through the grinder twice. Knead into a ball adding 1 teaspoon lemon rind, 1 teaspoon lemon juice and 1 tablespoon orange juice, then 2 tablespoons confectioners' sugar. Use more confectioners' sugar if needed to make a firm mass. Form into small balls and roll in granulated sugar. Allow to dry for several hours before storing.

APRICOT ORANGE BALLS

1 pound dried apricots   1 seedless orange
2 cups granulated sugar

Wash and dry 1 pound of apricots. Cut a whole seedless orange into pieces and grind finely with the apricots. Add 2 cups sugar and put the mixture into the top of a double boiler. Steam and stir until the sugar is well dissolved — about 10 minutes. Cool and shape the candy into small balls, roll in granulated sugar and let dry. Roll again in a few hours if they are too moist.

CANDIED ORANGE PEEL

Peel from 4 medium-sized   2 cups sugar
oranges   ¾ cup water
½ cup sugar

Remove the peel from 4 oranges carefully and cut into ¼-inch strips. Cover with cold water and bring to a boil. Cook slowly for 15 minutes, drain off water and repeat until peel is tender.

Blend 2 cups sugar and ¾ cup water in a 1-quart saucepan and bring to a boil. Put in your thermometer and boil quickly to 238°. Lower heat and add orange peel. Cook slowly until peel absorbs most of the liquid and begins to look transparent. Remove from heat and drop peel onto a pan over which has been spread a half cup of sugar. Roll until each piece is covered.

Grapefruit and lemon peel may be prepared the same way.

STUFFED APRICOTS or PRUNES

Steam apricots or prunes for 15 minutes until they are tender and plumped out. Cool and stuff with nut fondant, softened marshmallow or with marzipan.

STUFFED DATES

Wash and stone dates if necessary, stuff with fondant, walnuts or toasted almonds. These may then be dipped in chocolate.

CANDIED APRICOTS or PRUNES

1 pound dried prunes or apricots	1 cup sugar
	1½ cups water

Cook 1 pound dried prunes or apricots in 1 cup sugar blended with 1½ cups water over low heat in a covered 2-quart saucepan for about 30 minutes, watching carefully so that they do not burn. These may be used as they are, or they may be stuffed as above.

SUGARED NUTS

1½ cups sugar   ½ cup water
2 cups nutmeats

Measure 1½ cups sugar and ½ cup water into a small saucepan. Stir and blend until syrup boils, then put in your thermometer and cook to 240°. Add

almond

2 cups nuts and remove from heat. Stir until syrup is cloudy and begins to sugar. Turn out on greased platter and separate with fingers. As a variation use the water from the first cooking of orange peel in the

recipe for candied orange peel. Or the sugar that remains in the pan after finishing the candied peel may be diluted and recooked and the nuts added.

GLACÉED NUTS

2 cups sugar	¼ teaspoon cream of tartar
⅔ cup water	1 pound of nuts

Blend 2 cups sugar and ⅔ cup water in a 2-quart saucepan and dissolve over low heat, stirring continuously. When the syrup boils, add ¼ teaspoon cream of tartar and put in your candy thermometer. Wash away sugar crystals as they form with a brush or fork wrapped in muslin and dipped in hot water. Cook without stirring until 300° is reached. Remove from direct heat and put over boiling water to prevent hardening. Drop nuts in the syrup a few at a time and pick them out one by one with a fork. Place each nut separately on a greased pan or platter, allowing as little extra syrup as possible to cling to them. Stir the syrup no more than necessary or it may crystallize. Fruits may be glacéed by the same method. Instead of cream of tartar, 1 or 2 tablespoons of corn syrup may be used. Glacéed nuts do not keep long and are difficult to make in humid or rainy weather.

COCONUT MARSHMALLOW DIPS

16 commercial marshmallows
or 1 cup homemade
marshmallow
(1 tablespoon water with
commercial marsh-
mallows)

Walnut halves, steamed
apricots or bits of prune,
or dates
1 cup dry coconut

Melt 16 commercial marshmallows in a double boiler with 1 tablespoon water, or melt one cup of homemade marshmallow — no water needed. Dip nutmeats, steamed apricot halves or bits of prune in marshmallow and roll in coconut. Dates may also be used.

CARAMELS

Once there was a little girl who asked her mother if they might make some caramels.

"Goodness, no, child," her mother replied. "It takes forever to make caramels and we're going to have dinner in an hour or two."

By old methods caramels did take so long to make that hungry young cooks were likely to eat them before they had been cooked enough to harden properly. Some recipes we tried out took as long as three hours to cook.

This is chiefly because the milk or cream usually

used in caramels is apt to scorch easily — even with frequent stirring the heat must be kept low. Thus the time required to cook the mixture down to the proper consistency and up to the proper temperature drags on and on.

The secret of quick caramels is a simple one. The sugar and syrup are cooked to a very high temperature before adding the butter, milk and cream, which are then added bit by bit and bubble up and evaporate quickly. The caramels taste better cooked this way because long cooking of milk or cream tends to toughen candy and often causes curdling. If evaporated milk is used this method is not necessary because half the moisture has been removed from the milk already and it will cook quickly anyway.

Caramels are one of the top-favorite candies. Even poor-grade commercial caramels have their following. But if you have never eaten homemade caramels made with butter and heavy cream you don't know how good caramels can really be. They are among the easiest of candies to make, but again a candy thermometer is of prime importance. If you must make a batch of caramels before you get your thermometer, check the chart showing cold-water tests for various degrees and stages of candy cooking.

Autumn Holidays

The final temperature for cooking caramels depends on how hard and chewy you like them — as well as on the altitude and the weather of the place you are cooking them. We suggest temperatures of between 246° and 250° for sea level; but for a very hard caramel it is possible to go to 255° or 260°. The British like their caramels cooked to 270° or 280° where they are almost too hard to be chewed and must be sucked first.

If you like a fudgy-textured caramel, beat the caramels for a minute or two after adding the flavoring and before pouring into the pans.

Pans for caramels should be lightly buttered. If you forget to do this you will have real trouble trying to get them out. But all need not be lost! Heat the bottom of the pan slightly over a stove burner and you will be able to turn them out. A large heavy knife is best for cutting caramels. Mark the oblong or square of caramels lightly with the knife to be sure of uniformity, then cut through with one heavy slice. Cut your waxed paper or cellophane into sizes just large enough so that you can get a fold at the top and fold over the ends. Caramels should be wrapped soon after they are cut.

Caramels keep well — preferably in a cool place as

The Holiday Candy Book

with all candy — and taste even better the second or third day than the first. But like any homemade candy without preservatives, they are best eaten while comparatively fresh.

Our favorite recipe of the ones that follow is the cream caramel but we think the milk caramel an unusually good inexpensive candy.

CREAM CARAMELS

2 cups sugar	2 cups heavy cream
1 cup light corn syrup	(warmed)
¼ cup butter	½ teaspoon salt
2 teaspoons vanilla	

Measure 2 cups sugar and 1 cup light corn syrup into a 4-quart saucepan. Blend with a wooden spoon, and place over a low heat, stirring continuously until the thick mixture begins to dissolve. Continue stirring until the mixture boils, then put in your candy thermometer and boil without stirring over a high flame until the thermometer registers 305°. Have ready ¼ cup butter which has been broken into small pieces and 2 cups heavy cream which has been warmed. Remove the candy from the stove for only a moment, put in the first bit of butter, return the pan to the stove and continue cooking, stirring well and adding bits of butter. The mixture will bubble up and steam. Add 2 cups heavy cream slowly, never allowing the candy to stop boiling hard and continuing to stir vigorously so that it will not stick or burn. Continue cooking until the thermometer registers 246° to 250°, depending on how hard you wish the caramels to be. This whole process should not take more than 30 minutes and will usually take less if the heat is kept high enough. When the desired degree is reached remove the pan from the stove immediately. Let stand 5 minutes, add ½ teaspoon salt and 2 teaspoons vanilla. Stir only enough to blend, then pour into a lightly greased pan – 8 by 11 inches is a good size – and allow to cool for several hours. Turn out of the pan, cut into squares or oblongs with a heavy knife, wrap in waxed paper or moistureproof cellophane and store in a tin box. Caramels keep well for weeks in a cool place if they are not exposed to other types of candy.

CHOCOLATE CREAM CARAMELS

Follow recipe for cream caramels, only decrease the butter to 2 tablespoons and after the caramels are cooked stir in immediately 2 squares of melted bitter chocolate.

NUT CREAM CARAMELS

Let either cream caramels or chocolate cream caramels stand an extra 5 minutes after the vanilla is added and then stir in gently ½ to 1 cup of coarsely broken nutmeats — pecans, walnuts, black walnuts, brazil nuts or toasted blanched almonds.

MILK CARAMELS

2 cups sugar	2 cups warmed milk
1 cup light corn syrup	½ teaspoon salt
¼ cup butter	1 teaspoon vanilla

Measure 2 cups sugar and 1 cup light corn syrup into a 4-quart saucepan. Blend with a wooden spoon and stir over low heat until the thick mixture dissolves and comes to a boil. Put in your candy thermometer and cook without stirring over high heat until thermometer registers 305°. Have ready ¼ cup butter broken into bits and 2 cups warmed milk. Remove the pan from the stove for a moment, add the first bit of butter. Return to high heat immediately and continue cooking and stirring while adding the rest of the butter and the milk bit by bit. The mixture will bubble up and steam. Do not allow mixture to stop boiling. When the thermometer reaches 246° to 250°, depending on the hardness you wish, remove

from heat, let stand 5 minutes, add ½ teaspoon salt
and 1 teaspoon vanilla and pour into a buttered pan,
8 by 8 inches. Let cool for several hours, then turn
out and cut into squares. Because of the higher water
content in the milk, this caramel takes a little longer
to cook than do cream caramels or those made with
evaporated or condensed milk — up to 35 minutes by
this method.

CHOCOLATE MILK CARAMELS

Follow recipe for milk caramels, stirring in 2
squares of melted chocolate immediately after remov-
ing from heat.

NUT MILK CARAMELS

Add ½ to 1 cup broken nutmeats after caramels
have stood an extra 5 minutes.

EVAPORATED MILK CARAMELS

2 cups sugar	1 tall can (14½ ounces)
2 cups light corn syrup	evaporated milk
½ cup butter	1 teaspoon vanilla

Measure 2 cups sugar and 2 cups light corn syrup
into a 4-quart saucepan. Blend and stir over low heat
until mixture dissolves and begins to boil. Put in your

candy thermometer and boil rapidly over high heat, without stirring, to 250°. Have ready ½ cup butter broken into bits and 1 tall can evaporated milk at room temperature. Add the butter bit by bit and then the milk little by little, over high heat, stirring all the time. Do not let the mixture stop boiling. Continue to cook and stir over high heat until thermometer shows 244° to 248°, depending on hardness desired. Remove from heat, cool for 5 minutes and add 1 teaspoon vanilla, blending in gently. Then pour into a pan, 8 by 11 inches. Allow to cool several hours, then cut with a heavy knife into squares or oblongs. Wrap in waxed paper or moistureproof cellophane. Because these caramels are made with evaporated milk they cook quickly without taking the first mixture to a high temperature. For the same reason they harden at slightly lower temperature than do other caramels.

COFFEE CARAMELS

2 cups sugar	2 tablespoons butter
½ cup light corn syrup	1½ cups warmed cream
½ cup strong coffee	½ teaspoon salt
1 teaspoon vanilla	

Measure 2 cups sugar, ½ cup light corn syrup and ½ cup freshly made, strong coffee into a 3- or 4-quart saucepan. Blend with a wooden spoon and stir over low heat until the mixture dissolves and begins to boil. Put in your candy thermometer and continue boiling over high heat, until the thermometer reaches 280°, stirring occasionally. Have ready 2 tablespoons butter in bits and 1½ cups warmed cream. Add the butter bit by bit, stirring continuously, and then the cream little by little, never allowing the mixture to stop boiling. Continue to cook over high heat until the thermometer reads 246° to 250°. Let stand for 5 minutes, then add ½ teaspoon salt and 1 teaspoon vanilla, blending in gently, and pour into a buttered pan, 8 by 8 inches. Let cool for several hours then turn out and cut into squares or oblongs with a heavy knife. Wrap in waxed paper or moistureproof cellophane.

PENUCHE CARAMELS

1 cup sugar	½ cup butter
1 cup light brown sugar	1 cup warmed cream
1 cup light corn syrup	¼ teaspoon salt
2 teaspoons vanilla	

Measure 1 cup sugar, 1 cup light brown sugar and 1 cup light corn syrup into a 3- or 4-quart saucepan. Blend and stir over low heat until thick mixture dis-

solves and begins to boil. Put in your candy thermometer and boil rapidly over high heat until thermometer registers 305°. Have ready ½ cup butter
broken into bits and 1 cup cream which has been
warmed. Remove the pan from the heat for a moment, add the first bit of butter. Return to high heat
immediately and continue cooking and stirring while
adding the rest of the butter bit by bit and the cream
little by little. Do not allow the mixture to stop boiling. When the thermometer reaches 246° to 250°,
depending on the hardness you wish, remove from
heat and let stand 5 minutes. Then add ¼ teaspoon
salt and 2 teaspoons vanilla and pour into a pan,
8 by 8 inches. Let cool for several hours, then turn
out and cut into squares or oblongs.

CARAMEL APPLES

1 recipe milk caramels (*page 92*)
10 or 12 small to medium apples

Use the recipe for milk caramels, cooking the final
mixture to 246°. Pour the mixture into the top of a
double boiler and cool for 5 to 10 minutes. Place over
hot water. Medium-sized or small apples are best for
dipping. Wash, remove the stems and insert skewers
in 10 or 12 apples. Dip each apple into the caramel,

twirl, allow to drip, then set on heavy waxed paper and put into refrigerator immediately for 10 minutes. If caramel thickens and becomes too hard to handle, remelt over hot water.

CARAMEL PECAN TURTLES

1 recipe cream caramel
    (*page 90*)
½ pound pecans

1 pound sweet or semisweet
    chocolate

Make 1 recipe of cream caramels or evaporated milk caramels, cooking the final mixture to 246°. Place ½ pound pecan meats in little circles of 3 to 4 pecans on large greased cookie sheets. When the caramel has cooled for 10 minutes drop by spoonfuls on the circle of pecans. If you have one, you can use a metal funnel and wooden stick, only be sure to heat and oil both the funnel and stick. Pour the caramel into the funnel and push circlets of caramel out with the stick.

Put cookie sheets into the refrigerator to cool for about 15 minutes.

Meanwhile melt 1 pound sweet or semisweet chocolate over hot (not boiling) water, stirring and beating while melting it. Remove from water before chocolate is completely melted and continue beating until chocolate is all melted and has begun to cool.

When it is just cool to the touch drop the caramel turtles into the chocolate, pick up with fingers or fork and set on waxed paper to cool. Or dip turtle only halfway into chocolate.

For more detailed instructions on melting chocolate see section on chocolate dipping, pages 32–37.

LAYER CARAMELS

Use any preferred recipe for caramels, using two pans instead of one so that the caramels will be thin enough to use in layers. For marshmallow layers melt either homemade or commercial marshmallows over hot water, being careful not to get the marshmallow too hot and runny. Remove from heat as soon as all lumps are out. Turn caramel out of pans, spread marshmallow mixture over one layer of caramel. Set in refrigerator for 10 minutes; then place second layer of caramel on top. Return to refrigerator for 10 minutes more; then set in a cool place. Cut in squares and wrap immediately in waxed paper or cellophane so that caramels will not spread. For fig-filled caramels use recipe for fig filling and spread that over one layer of caramel, putting other layer on top.

Two different kinds of caramels may be put together also.

FIG FILLING

½ pound figs   ½ cup water
1 cup sugar   2 tablespoons lemon juice

Wash ½ pound figs thoroughly, dry them and put through a food chopper. Measure 1 cup sugar and ½ cup water in a 1-quart saucepan, blend and stir over low heat until sugar dissolves and syrup boils. Cook to 275° without stirring. Remove from heat and pour over ground figs, stirring thoroughly; set mixture over hot water to dry out. After half an hour add 2 tablespoons lemon juice and stir. Continue to dry out for another 20 minutes. Cool before using.

Children's Candies

CANDY and children are an inseparable combination, particularly if the candy is taffy. Letting the youngsters help make candy may be hard on the nerves, but it's warming to the heart.

Some of the candies in this section can be made by children but all of them are to be made *for* children. Lollipops are a pretty fussy job for youngsters although they might enjoy trying to write their names on one. Popcorn balls are easier. They can at least pop the corn and form the balls. Hard candies are too hot to handle for most youngsters but they all love barley sugar and candy sticks and spirals.

Taffy is ideal. A children's party that includes a taffy pull is bound to be a success and — if you and your kitchen can stand it — a lot of fun for the adults present too. The taffy is not apt to be of the best when it is finished and most of it will be in or on the children before that times comes.

While it is best to pull taffy with fingers which

have been dampened with cold water or dusted with cornstarch, children seem to have a better time when they butter their fingers and also seem to feel the warmth less. All of the taffies given here are cooked to a fairly low temperature and can be pulled until they are quite cold. If the adults present do the early pulling and then divide up the candy among the children to pull, no one will get burned fingers.

CANDY APPLES ON A STICK

2 cups light brown sugar
2/3 cup water
1 tablespoon light corn syrup

1/2 teaspoon lemon extract
6 to 8 apples and sticks

Measure 2 cups light brown sugar, 2/3 cup water and 1 tablespoon light corn syrup into a small saucepan. A small, deep pan is good here for complete submerging of the apple in the hot syrup. Blend mixture well with a wooden spoon and place over heat, stirring until all the sugar is dissolved. When candy boils, put in the candy thermometer and continue boiling without stirring. When the thermometer registers 290°, remove candy from heat and measure in 1/2 teaspoon lemon extract. Let the bubbles subside and then put the first apple into the saucepan. Have ready a pan of icy-cold water and quickly plunge the coated apple into the ice water. Allow to remain in only long enough to solidify the taffy coating. Drain on a dampened cloth and place on a buttered pan. Dipping of the apples without the aid of the chilled water to hasten the hardening process may be done. There will be an accumulation of syrup where the apple is placed on the buttered pan but to some of us this is the trademark of a homemade taffy apple.

MOLASSES–TAFFY KISSES

½ cup brown sugar	½ cup water
1 cup granulated sugar	¼ cup butter
¾ cup *light* molasses	½ teaspoon each of vanilla,
½ cup milk	salt and soda
¾ cup dark corn **syrup**	Pinch of cream of tartar

Measure into a saucepan and blend well: ½ cup brown sugar, 1 cup granulated sugar, ¾ cup light molasses, ½ cup milk, ¾ cup dark corn syrup, ½ cup water, ¼ cup butter. Place over medium heat and stir occasionally to keep from sticking. When mixture boils put in the candy thermometer and continue to boil until the thermometer registers 254°. Remove from heat and gently stir in ½ teaspoon each of vanilla, salt and soda, and a pinch of cream of tartar.

The last ingredient is added to bleach the candy somewhat. Pour the hot syrup on a buttered platter or large pan and allow to cool until it can be handled. As it cools fold the edges into the center and then take the whole amount of candy and pull and stretch for several minutes. When it is light and fluffy, twist it into lengths and cut into pieces. Since this recipe gives a soft and chewy candy it must be wrapped, each piece separately. Moistureproof cellophane is ideal if obtainable, though waxed paper can be used. Cornstarch or butter can be used on the fingers when pulling the candy. It is important to use light molasses in this recipe because the flavor of the dark is too strong and often bitter.

SALT–WATER TAFFY

2 cups sugar	2 tablespoons butter
1¼ cups corn syrup	Flavoring and coloring as
¾ cup water	desired
1 teaspoon salt	

Measure 2 cups sugar, 1¼ cups corn syrup, ¾ cup water, 1 teaspoon salt into a saucepan and blend well with a wooden spoon. Place over low heat until sugar has dissolved, stirring continuously. Increase the heat and do not stir during the rest of the cooking. Wash the sides of the pan with a brush or fork covered with muslin and dipped in water, using an upward motion. This will prevent the formation of crystals which might cause the candy to sugar. After the syrup boils put in the candy thermometer, and when the thermometer registers 265°, remove candy from heat.

Add 2 tablespoons butter and stir very gently. If only white vanilla-flavored candy is desired, pour the candy onto one large buttered platter. Sprinkle with 1 teaspoon vanilla after it has cooled. The flavor will work through when it is pulled. A variety of colors and flavors may be had by dividing into three parts. Color one pink by adding a few drops of red coloring and ⅓ teaspoon raspberry flavoring. Color the second yellow and add ⅓ teaspoon of lemon extract. Leave

Children's Candies

the third white and flavor with either ⅓ teaspoon vanilla or ¼ teaspoon mint. Children enjoy the different colors and it is well worth the extra trouble of pulling three separate parts. In fact pulling taffy, making popcorn balls and taffy apples where the children participated was the success of a recent holiday party. When the candy was divided three of the children were given a color to pull. When the candy becomes light in color and texture it is stretched out into lengths and cut into pieces which are individually wrapped.

MAPLE TAFFY

1 cup maple syrup	¼ teaspoon cream of tartar
1 cup sugar	½ tablespoon vinegar
	1 tablespoon butter

Measure 1 cup maple syrup and 1 cup sugar into a saucepan and blend together with a wooden spoon. Place over low heat until the sugar and syrup comes to a boil, stirring well. Stir in ¼ teaspoon cream of tartar which has been mixed with ½ tablespoon vinegar. Next add 1 tablespoon butter and allow the mixture to boil without stirring. At this point put in the candy thermometer, and when the thermometer registers 260° remove from heat. Pour onto a buttered platter or large pan to cool. As the edges of the candy cool fold toward the center. When the whole mass is cool enough to handle take it up and pull, using the tips of the fingers as much as possible. It will be quite light in color when finished. Roll the candy into strips and cut into pieces. Because of the maple syrup this taffy has a tendency to sugar when a few days old. It is just as delicious, for the texture is very fine grained and smooth to the taste.

CHOCOLATE POPCORN NUT CLUSTERS

3 one-ounce cakes sweet
   chocolate
2 tablespoons rich cream

2 cups popped corn
1 cup pecans (broken into
   small pieces)

Melt 3 ounces sweet chocolate over hot water. Slowly and carefully add 2 tablespoons rich cream and mix together. Pour this over 2 cups popcorn and 1 cup chopped pecans that have been mixed well together. Spoon out in small clusters on waxed paper and let dry.

BARLEY CANDY TWISTS

2 cups light corn syrup   2 cups sugar
½ cup water

Measure 2 cups light corn syrup, 2 cups sugar and ½ cup water into a saucepan and blend well together.

Place over low heat and stir until mixture boils. Now put in the candy thermometer and continue boiling without stirring until candy thermometer registers 310°. Cooking this syrup rapidly at the end caramelizes the syrup and adds a golden color to the candy. Pour on a buttered platter and when still warm cut into small pieces and twist each piece. This candy must be kept in a dry, airtight container.

LOLLIPOPS, CANDY STICKS AND SPIRALS

Using the hard-candy recipe (see pages 73–74) many varieties of children's candies may be made. The syrup is cooked to 300°, then colored and flavored depending on the type of candy to be formed. Lollipops are a great favorite with all children and can be flavored lemon, orange, peppermint, anise, raspberry and strawberry. These flavors can be obtained in most food stores. They are extracts and a whole recipe requires 1 teaspoon. If oil flavors are used, a few drops of peppermint, wintergreen or cinnamon are all that are required for a whole recipe. Vegetable colorings are best and the amount used is, of course, dependent upon the intensity of the color desired. Pink will require a very little amount of the red, and green should be very carefully used as this color is much more attractive if it is kept light. Wooden skewers may be obtained from the butcher and used for the handles of the lollipops. The candy is either poured out in circles or spooned out on a flat buttered surface. Before the circles harden, the skewer is firmly

placed in the candy. The decoration can be planned to fit any holiday or party occasion. Lollipops can be used as place cards for a children's party. Royal icing (see page 29) is pressed from a pastry tube to form the name of each child. The fine attachment is best for this and with a little practice you will find it easy to write the names in a script style. Names and initials may also be put on the lollipops with another pastry-tube attachment that will also form a ribbon border around the edge. There are many other attachments for the pastry tube which you can experiment with to get additional ideas for decorating. Faces, flowers and holiday motifs can be worked out in many different ways. Once you use this special royal icing in

the pastry tube, the hidden artist in you will take over and the results will delight the children. Raisins, nuts, coconut and pieces of fruit can also be used for decorating, but this must be done while the candy is warm. Raisins for eyes, a piece of nut for the nose, a piece of cherry for the mouth and coconut for the hair make an effective face.

Candy sticks are made using the same basic hard-candy recipe. The colors and flavors are a matter of choice, and if several varieties are to be made the candy is divided on plates and worked separately. If this is the case it is well to keep the candy warm until you are ready to form it in sticks. While the candy is still warm it is cut into pieces and each piece is rolled separately to form a stick. The rolling is continued until the candy is cool enough to keep its shape and then is placed in a cool room. When all the sticks are formed and well cooled, keep them in an airtight container, as all hard candies readily absorb moisture if left exposed to the air.

Spirals are another attractive hard candy. The basic hard-candy recipe is followed and the candy is divided into three portions. The first is flavored with peppermint and left uncolored. The second is flavored with raspberry and colored red. The third is flavored with wintergreen and colored green. The flavors and coloring must be very carefully and gently worked into the hot syrup, for too much stirring will cause the syrup to sugar. Heat your oven in order to keep the candy warm while some portions are being shaped. About one half a teaspoonful of the candy is taken and rolled into a long rope, and this is then quickly wrapped round and round a wooden skewer that has been well greased. The spiral is slipped off and set to cool and another is formed. It is important to work fast once the candy is removed from the warmth of the oven.

Making Candy in Large Quantities

MANY candies can be made successfully at home in fairly large quantities, without any more special equipment than an extra-large kettle. Others need big beaters, large marble-top tables, or other special equipment, such as candy bars, cutters, candy hooks, batch warmers and so on, which are only worth the investment if you mean to set up a small candy factory.

If you are interested in making candies in comparatively large quantities either for gifts for church bazaars or for sale, you will need to choose your types of candy.

Caramels are easy to cook in large batches, but are a chore to cut and wrap. Fondant is also easy to cook in a large batch but you will need a large enough slab to cool it all at once since you cannot be creaming three or four platters or pans at the same time.

For fudge, the beating of large quantities is the

Making Candy in Large Quantities

chief difficulty. Size of beater bowls will keep you from making more than the regular recipes for nougats, marshmallows and divinity. Butter crunch is best made in small quantities but several batches may be made in succession and the chocolate coating done all at once.

Hard candies are too difficult to handle to make more than a small quantity at a time unless you are simply pouring it into pans and cutting it into squares. For lollipops, candy sticks and other varieties that have to be formed, it is too difficult to keep the candy from hardening to make large-quantity cooking attractive.

Suggested extra equipment for the cook who wants to make a great deal of candy are a large marble slab, a large-size electric mixer, a candy hook for pulling taffy in quantity, and rubber mats and starch trays for molding fondant and jellies as well as crystallizing racks and trays for bonbons.

Sometimes caramels and nougats are difficult to remove from a pan. Useful to anyone who makes these candies are the metal, ¾-inch candy bars, with the length cut to order. When these are set on a marble slab the candy can be poured in and the bars removed easily after it is set. The bars too, will give straight edges and sharp corners to every piece, though the cutting of the long strips into individual pieces will have to be done by hand.

Any recipe in this book may be doubled or tripled without causing too much trouble for the candy cook. Saucepan sizes will need to be at least half again as large for most double batches and more than twice as large for triple batches, particularly for candies that are boiled briskly and contain cream or milk or butter.

Included here are some special extra-large recipes for candies that can be handled in quantity.

FONDANT

5 pounds sugar   3½ cups hot water
½ teaspoon cream of tartar

Measure 5 pounds (10 cups) sugar into an 8-quart saucepan with 3½ cups hot water and ½ teaspoon cream of tartar. Follow general directions for fondant (see pages 19–27). Pour out on large marble slab and work when cool. For butter creams add ½ pound soft butter before creaming.

Making Candy in Large Quantities

CREAM CARAMELS

3 pounds sugar	6 cups warmed cream
2 pounds light corn syrup	1 teaspoon salt
¾ cup butter	2 tablespoons vanilla

Measure into an 8-quart saucepan 3 pounds (6 cups) sugar, 2 pounds (3 cups) light corn syrup. Blend and boil to 305°, then add ¾ cup butter in pieces and 6 cups warmed cream. Cook to 246° to 250° and let stand 5 minutes, then add 1 teaspoon salt and 2 tablespoons vanilla. Pour into three pans, 8 by 11 inches, or between caramel bars set at 15 inches square. When set and cool remove bars and cut in squares or oblongs. For more detailed directions see regular recipe for cream caramels (pages 90–91).

PEANUT BRITTLE

3 pounds sugar	¼ cup butter
2 pounds light corn syrup	6 cups salted peanuts
1 cup hot water	3 teaspoons baking soda
1 teaspoon vanilla	

Measure into a 6-quart saucepan 3 pounds (6 cups) sugar, 2 pounds (3 cups) light corn syrup and 1 cup hot water. Blend and boil to 280°, then add

¼ cup butter and 6 cups salted peanuts. Continue cooking to 300°, remove from heat, add 3 teaspoons soda and stir well, then add 1 teaspoon vanilla. Pour thinly into five or six large buttered pans or trays and stretch and turn the candy as it cools.

INDEX

Index

NOTE: Page numbers on which recipes occur are set in boldface type.

Index

Index

Index

Index

Thanksgiving, 3, 81
Thermometer, 8, 12–13
    correcting for altitude, 13
    correcting for humid or
      rainy weather, 13
    reading, 12
    testing, 12
Toffee, 7, 11, 37, 72, **79**
Truffles, Hazelnut, **37–38**
Turkish Paste, 64, 67
Turtles, Caramel Pecan, **97–98**

Twists, **107–111**. *See also*
    Basic Hard Candy,
    73–74
    Barley Candy, **106–107**

WALNUTS
    in Coconut Marshmallow
      Dips, 87
    in Stuffed Dates, 84
Washington's Birthday, 17
Weddings, 60
Winter holidays, 16–40

[123]

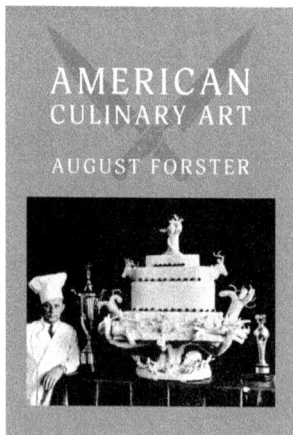

AMERICAN
CULINARY ART
AUGUST FORSTER

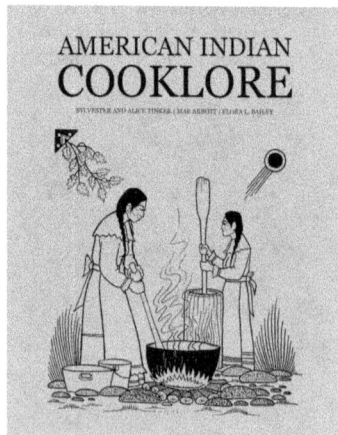

AMERICAN INDIAN
COOKLORE
SYLVESTER AND ALICE TINKER / MAE ABBOTT / FLORA L. BAILEY

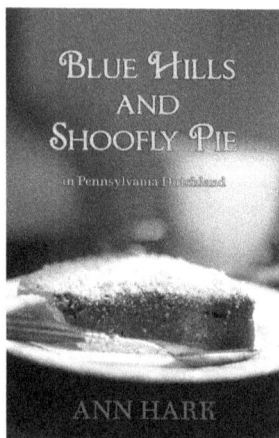

BLUE HILLS
AND
SHOOFLY PIE
in Pennsylvania Dutchland

ANN HARK

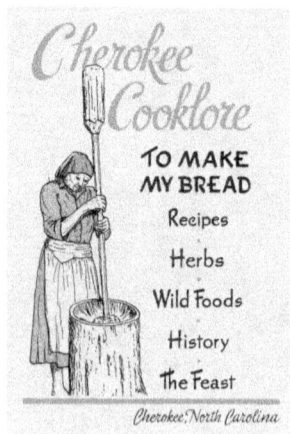

Cherokee
Cooklore
TO MAKE
MY BREAD
Recipes
Herbs
Wild Foods
History
The Feast
Cherokee, North Carolina

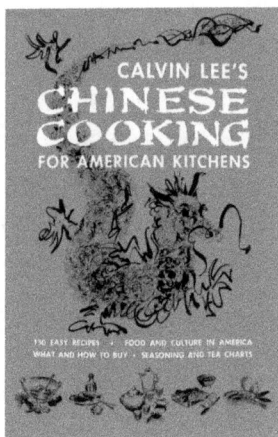

CALVIN LEE'S
CHINESE
COOKING
FOR AMERICAN KITCHENS

130 EASY RECIPES · FOOD AND CULTURE IN AMERICA
WHAT AND HOW TO BUY · SEASONING AND TEA CHARTS

BETTY
ROSELLA

COOKERY
MUSHROOM

Pennsylvania
German
Cookery

A REGIONAL COOKBOOK BY
ANN HARK & PRESTON A. BARBA

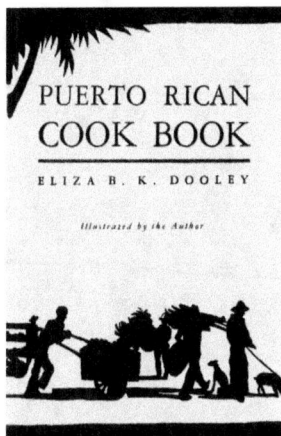

PUERTO RICAN
COOK BOOK

ELIZA B. K. DOOLEY

Illustrated by the Author

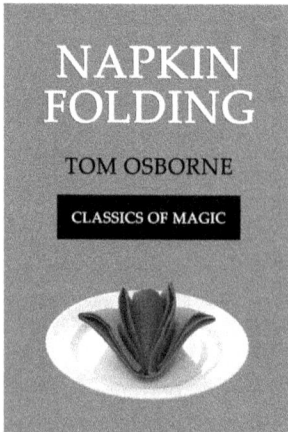

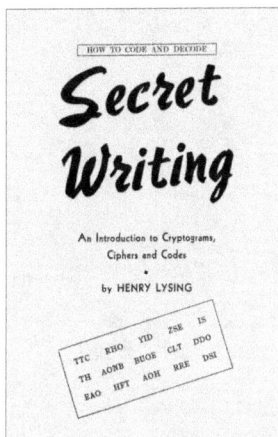

HOW TO CODE AND DECODE

Secret Writing

An Introduction to Cryptograms,
Ciphers and Codes
•
by HENRY LYSING

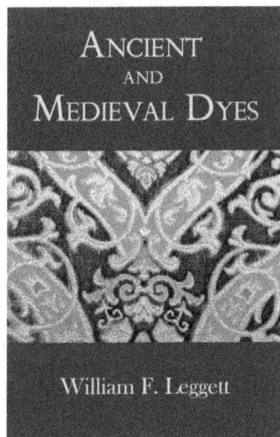

ANCIENT
AND
MEDIEVAL DYES

William F. Leggett

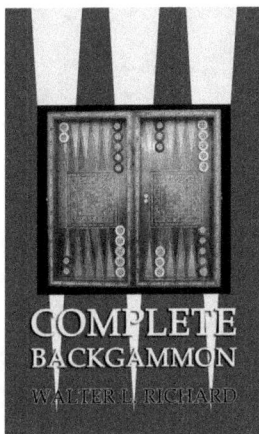

COMPLETE
BACKGAMMON
WALTER L. RICHARD

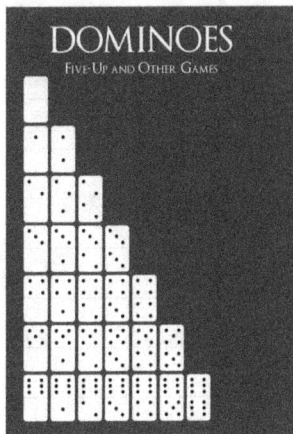

DOMINOES
FIVE-UP AND OTHER GAMES

www.ingramcontent.com/pod-product-compliance
Lightning Source LLC
LaVergne TN
LVHW021507080426
835509LV00018B/2434